"Christianity and the Family" comprises the Rauschenbusch Lectures, given at the Colgate-Rochester Divinity School. It is a stirring plea for a more universal Christian interest in the family, and a keen analysis of its problems in modern society.

In the first part of this book, Dr. Groves demonstrates the emphasis which Jesus placed on the alliance between the family and the church as basic institutions. Christ's constant message was based upon family experience and delivered in family vocabulary. The second part of the book deals with the responsibilities of the Christian ministry and the unfolding opportunities for a successful program to strengthen the nation's marital and family bonds.

"Christianity and the Family" contains a wealth of practical help gained from the author's years of experience in dealing with the domestic problems of countless men and women who have sought his aid. It is an invaluable handbook for family counselling and in preaching on the problems of the Christian family.

THE MACMILLAN COMPANY
NEW YORK · BOSTON · CHICAGO · DALLAS
ATLANTA · SAN FRANCISCO

MACMILLAN AND CO., Limited
LONDON · BOMBAY · CALCUTTA · MADRAS
MELBOURNE

THE MACMILLAN COMPANY
OF CANADA, Limited
TORONTO

CHRISTIANITY AND THE FAMILY

by

Ernest R. Groves

New York

THE MACMILLAN COMPANY

1942

PRINTED IN THE UNITED STATES OF AMERICA

FOREWORD

FOR many years I have been deeply interested in the relationship between religion and American home life. Undoubtedly the home as an institution and marriage as a relationship are subjected to heavy antagonisms and tensions in our modern world. Those of us who have been watching the effects of these influences on home life have a sense of profound responsibility to bring such values as we may have to the support of these institutions. It is for this reason that religious leaders have turned with deep interest to the field of the home.

All who are interested in the church recognize also that in a real sense the home is the institution which determines the kind of persons emerging into society who can build a useful church. Without the undergirding of the home the church is greatly handicapped in the work it can do. To all of us thus situated it has been a source of great satisfaction to see different educational institutions become centers of research and intelligent social inquiry into the functions of home life, and we have been particularly glad to see institutions of learning undertake to prepare students for marriage and the home experience as definitely as they prepare them for other important relationships.

Among those who have seen this opportunity and

obligation, Dr. Groves, of Chapel Hill, has been one of the pioneers. It has been true that for a number of years the literature coming from his hands and the research data gathered at Chapel Hill from conferences and other inquiries associated with his department have been both influential and stimulating to all who sought constructive answers to the problems in this area. Quite a time ago when the committee on the Rauschenbusch Foundation of The Colgate-Rochester Divinity School was considering the various areas of American life in which the social principles underlying the Christian religion should function, they faced this growing recognition on the part of the church to its obligation to the home and invited Dr. Groves to be the lecturer. Much of the material of this book was used in lectures given at the Institution in the spring of 1941. It has been supplemented further by other material which combines to form the book which is here presented. The School is glad to see the book come to the attention of the public, commends it to all who are interested in this phase of our modern life and hopes that the ideas here set forth may prove stimulating and challenging enough to those who read to result in their passing them along to individuals and groups who are interested and responsible for the relation of religion to this field of home and marriage.

ALBERT W. BEAVEN, *President*

The Colgate-Rochester Divinity School

PREFACE

Christianity and the Family is a plea to the Protestant ministry for a more practical, understanding interest in the family and a greater appreciation of its relation to Christianity. The clergy are not lacking in concern for the welfare of marriage and the family, but they, like other people, are too apt to be content with spasmodic, occasional efforts to conserve the family instead of planning and carrying out a detailed, deliberate program. A sentimental attitude toward domestic relations, that is not translated into concrete activity, does not go far in helping a family to fulfill its spiritual mission.

The book is divided into two parts. The first attempts to bring forth the significance of the family for the Christian way of life. Christianity is regarded as more normally close to wholesome family life than any other religious faith. The thesis of this section of the book is that Jesus recognized this alliance that should be maintained between the family and the church and that he made use of family experience and its vocabulary as a means of unfolding his message. In order to get at the meaning of the family in the spiritual life of our day, the appearance of asceticism in Christian dogma and practice and the social conditions of contemporary American society that hamper the spiritual functioning of the family are also discussed.

The next section is concerned with the responsibilities and opportunities of the minister for a program directed toward strengthening marriage and the family. The minister's rôle as a teacher and as a counselor is stressed. The book seeks to give confidence to the minister who tries to help the family perform its spiritual purposes, to aid him in both his teachings and his counseling, and to warn him of and safeguard him from the hazards associated with his pastoral services as a counselor. I have the conviction that the professional experiences of the pastor can furnish a large part of the preparation needed for a skillful, helpful counseling service. In the writing of the book, I have drawn upon more than thirty years of constant contact with domestic problems brought by men and women who have asked for help in the handling of their troubles.

I wish to acknowledge the inspiration I had for the writing of this book through my appointment as Lecturer on the Rauschenbusch Foundation at Colgate-Rochester Divinity School in the spring of 1941. Especially do I wish to thank President Albert William Beaven of that Institution, my colleague, Donald S. Klaiss, University of North Carolina, my wife, Gladys Hoagland Groves, for their suggestions; the last, for her critical reading of the manuscript, and to Mrs. Sally Denton Coe for her care and interest in preparing it for the printer.

E. R. G.

Chapel Hill, North Carolina
September 1, 1941

CONTENTS

		PAGE
FOREWORD		v
PREFACE		vii

PART I

The Family As An Ally of Christianity

CHAPTER

I. THE FAMILY AS THE ALLY OF CHRISTI-	
ANITY	3
II. THE SPIRITUAL FUNCTION OF THE FAMILY	22
III. CHRISTIANITY AND SEX	37
IV. THE FAMILY AND CHRISTIAN CHARACTER	65
V. HAMPERING CONDITIONS AND TRADITIONS	79

PART II

The Church As An Ally of the Family

VI. THE CHURCH AND EDUCATION FOR FAMILY	
LIFE	105
VII. THE MINISTER AS A DOMESTIC COUN-	
SELOR	128
VIII. THE RÔLES OF THE DOMESTIC COUNSELOR	142
IX. THE ART OF DOMESTIC COUNSELING . .	162
X. THE HAZARDS OF DOMESTIC COUNSELING	202
BIBLIOGRAPHY	221
INDEX	225

PART I

THE FAMILY AS AN ALLY OF CHRISTIANITY

CHAPTER I

The Family As the Ally of Christianity

THE importance of the family is universally recognized. Like most supremely significant facts, its significance is taken for granted. This is so true that any attempt to establish its position as a social institution seems to thoughtful people a waste of words. We have to stress its value by directing attention to something that it does. We choose one of its many activities and interpret this as it appears in some particular instance, thus getting an inkling of its resources of power and influence.

To define it as a chief social institution is not enough to make us realize how much it does in its ministration to human needs. Such a verbal statement seems abstract and conceals the intricate and subtle ways the family operates. We do not warm up to any portrayal of the family functioning unless we are permitted to glimpse what it does to and for people. To get this insight we have to look at the family in action.

When we try to get at the meaning of the family for Christianity, we find ourselves in the same situation. If we insist the family is the social institution most valuable as an ally of Christianity, our assertion is accepted by almost everybody, but unless we go further and illustrate this relationship as it is expressed in concrete, everyday occurrence, our statement becomes formal and logical but devoid of the appreciation that is necessary to persuade us of the naturalness and the necessity of the family and the Christian church being active partners each to the other. Unless the analysis of family functioning awakens emotion, the realness of what we are trying to discover slips from our understanding.

It is obvious that any social institution that has the influence possessed by the family would have some relationship to Christianity. This would also be true of any other religious faith. Domestic and religious interests so overlap that we can always assume an exchange of influences between them. There is, however, more than this ordinary relationship between the family and Christianity. The Christian faith emphasizes certain teachings that especially tie up with inherent experiences belonging to the normal home. It is in this special sense that the family can be regarded as an ally of Christianity. To do justice to this, we must examine the teachings of both Jesus and the church and trace in some detail their relation to the life of the wholesome home.

Although the many-sidedness of the teaching of Jesus is one of its most distinguishing characteristics and as a result there have been various choices in the selection of a core for his message, none seems so justly to uncover his way of life as his invitation to the believer to become a member of the household of God. This relationship was possessed by anyone who accepted the fatherhood of God and practiced the brotherhood of man. Jesus was convinced that the words that would best bring the meaning of his mission within the understanding of his followers had to come out of the life of the home. Nothing can so well uncover the importance of the family in the program of Christianity as this fact that Jesus needed to go to the vocabulary of family association for suggestive ideas that would have some hope of conveying the genius of his teaching to those who as co-workers were later to take over the task of a new spiritual crusade.

Jesus turned to family life not merely for the purpose of selecting words or illustrative examples, but even more to uncover the meaning of some of the happenings that were familiar memories of most of his hearers and apply them to spiritual experience. He knew that he was drawing from emotional material that was already recognized as powerful, for the significance of childhood, and its determining influence was appreciated in his day as in ours. He had the task of building new concepts of human life and a larger sense of social responsibility, and it was in the family that he found a foundation for this teaching in common everyday experiences that could be made use of as a basis for his new doctrines. Where else but in the life of the orthodox Jewish home could he find such an opportunity to gather ideas that would provide the insight needed?

The life motive sufficient for the Christian way of life was a spiritual kinship most nearly related to the love that appears among family members in the normal home. The Christian sentiment, to be sure, was not a mere extension of the feelings that give the family substance but the affection that has its being in household contacts was nevertheless suggestive of and in its essence preparatory to the achievement of the higher type of love.

There was nothing subtle or extraordinary in the description Jesus made of this commanding motive. Love gave the power that led to the keeping of the commandments. No philosophic background, no theological insight, not even a fortunate education was needed to get this significance of affection as a causal impulse because the propulsion of love was a familiar experience then as now, and was either found or profoundly craved in parent-child and husband-wife relationships. On a higher level, the moving force that was to insure loyalty, unity, and service was a commitment of affection suggested by the love that enabled family members to achieve domestic virtue.

Although love was interpreted as portraying the supreme achievement in the fellowship of God and man, it was not regarded as something extraordinary, an attainment beyond the power of the average men and women. His followers were not to regard it as an interpolation or an accretion grafted onto human nature, but rather as the flowering of normal human traits. At this point it was easy for misunderstanding to arise. Religious zeal is always open to the temptation to create ideals that are set apart from everyday life and that seem to gather their meaning from their peculiarity and estrangement from mundane affairs. This was not the point of view of Jesus but, in contrast, he wished to uncover the values, the satisfactions and the responsibilities that were inherently tied to any social brotherhood. His way of life drew its momentum from fellowship with God but expressed itself in ordinary everyday activities; in the spirit and motive of one's practices rather than in unusual, unnatural behavior.

In order to make this clear to his disciples, there was need of leading them to see the deeper meaning of social relationship, and from no place could the Master draw such resources for the enforcing of his teachings as from the religiously motivated homes of his people. Although realized in differing degrees by the various families, this spiritual achievement was, nevertheless, something that most parents knew at first hand or that they had come to appreciate from their childhood in their contact with their own parents. It was not an alien graft pushed into the family through social suggestion or the personal recognition of obligation. It was a quality that belonged normally to the association of parents and children. Indeed, then, as now, it was not too much to say that it was a domestic possession without which there would be serious emptiness in any home, even a hazardous deficiency because of the survival purpose of love. Parental affection replaced the instinct of the animal, the automatic endowment provided to enforce the care of offspring. It provided a more lasting force, a positive and creative attachment, and by its mere existence gave vitality to the parent-child association, so that the father and mother were not just more responsible guardians and caretakers. As parents they were given the opportunity to have a contact with the child that added a meaning to their ministration that was far removed from anything instinct can ever furnish.

It is important also in order to understand the genius of Jesus' teachings to notice that this was not something evoked in the parent by outside pressure. Even though we grant that the environment with its cultural standards and mass suggestions influenced the part that the parental service took, the motive, if it became mature and genuine parental affection, was something belonging to the inner life of the father and the mother. When this was not true, there was a deficiency in the relationship of the child and parent that the former sooner or later was bound to realize. This fact discloses how hopefully Jesus could turn the attention of his followers back to their own home life for the illustrative material he needed to clarify and enforce his message. His task would have been much more difficult had he been dealing with human nature that had never had the tutelage of domestic association.

The Christian life, however, was not merely the recognition of domestic relationship, since this easily becomes formal, cold, and static, but a feeling toward the fellowship that made it self-nourishing, progressive, and compelling. Such achievement would neither seem impossible nor mysterious to those who could draw from their own personal, domestic experience intimation of a heavenly fatherhood and a universal brotherhood.

No present love can insure future affection. As we experience love, it is time-tied. It moves forward not because it was once strong but on account of its power of self-renewal. This the parent comes to understand because progression is the supreme test of the vitality and the wholesomeness of any domestic fellowship. This onwardness of Christian living both of the individual and of the group that was so soon to become the church was the product, according to the teaching of Jesus, of a faith that maintained its initial love. Now that we look backward over the long, historic record of Christian experience, we can detect the naturalness of this forward-going so long as the essential element of the relationship was conceived in domestic symbols, and the difficulty of preventing the Christian goal from becoming formal, sterile, and stationary when the meaning of the fatherhood of God and the brotherhood of man was sought in a dogma and a status rather than through experiencing a fellowship of love.

These backward movements in the history of Christianity did more than register a lowering of the vitality of the church. In part, they revealed a desire to find an easier way of Christian living as a result of the temporary weakening of the faith. They were also, however, a turning off from the path of spiritual practice as a consequence of obtuseness. Most of all, they indicated a failure of vision. Practices and beliefs went

askew on account of a spiritual blindness as the energy
of the church began to ebb and, of course, this was
most apparent in the leadership.

Recourse was taken, as is always true in such circumstances, to a substitute that would give a semblance
of the original energy. This had to be something
mechanical that could be made a matter of routine. It
was natural in this predicament for both leaders and
followers to seek a formula for life that was static and
not too demanding, thus replacing dynamic, progressive, spiritual experience by a life-pattern that could
be cemented into a churchly code of behavior. Formal-
ism and doctrine gave fulfillment to this seeking by an
enfeebled Christianity. Escape from the ordeal of the
true following of Jesus is provided by ritual and
dogma. The first, lifeless when disassociated from inner
spiritual growth, and the other, a substitute for purposeful grappling with reality by ideas that have
a fictitious value and need not be expressed in action
in the world of ordinary life, fill the void created by
the passing of spiritual zeal and genuine fellowship in
the spirit of Jesus.

It is a betrayal of the deeper truths of the teaching
of Jesus to suppose that he merely made use of the
family experience as it was known by his disciples
for the sake of interpreting the message entrusted to
them. If we seek the reason for his use of the home
life of his time, it becomes clear that the family was
more than a mere explanation. In an elemental, everyday way it provided the tutelage that was necessary
for the understanding of the spirit of love as it flowed

from the fatherhood of God and expressed itself in the brotherhood of man. This teaching lifted the family out of a period of time and made it the source of a continuous Christian service.

This contribution of domestic experience is true for us, as it must be for our children's children, because as a means of implanting, nourishing, and maturing love and making it a foundation of a higher love of a superior order, the family still functions as a preparation, and there is nothing to encourage the idea that its function can be surrendered to any other institution or organization. As a consequence, the family is not merely a sphere of life where Christian motives are expressed, nor an obligation that Christian people are quick to accept, but a nurturing fellowship which brings forth impulses that can be spiritualized and made the substance of Christian experience. The humanizing that occurs through family contact becomes a tutelage for the spiritual development without which there can be no genuine following of the program of Jesus.

It is this preparatory functioning of the family that makes the home of such great importance to the church and the minister. The frail, the empty, and the debased families not only obstruct development of character, they deny during the formative period of the child the experiences that best provide the foundation for growth of Christian personality. This does not mean, of course, that family life necessarily produces religious or Christian development. There is no automatic flowering of domestic life which with certainty brings a child into the household of God, but on the other hand the wholesome attainments of family living bring an insight to the people of today —as was true in the time of Jesus—that uncovers the meaning of that kinship of affection which is the distinctive quality of the Christian way of life. The bad home or the unfortunate childhood does not render impossible a later Christian career, but it does create difficulties and in its essential functioning fails to contribute the values that belong to domesticity, and which normally support the later, adult spiritualizing of life.

We must, however, be cautious in our interpretation of the causal influences of childhood. There is no mechanical certainty of determination, operating so simply as to forecast the destination of the adult. Instead we find that the child has, himself, an active part in the final outcome and that his destitution emotionally, his failure to get adequate understanding or support from his parents, may create a realization of loss that in later life will increase his demands for affection or lead him to seek for others a greater opportunity than he himself enjoyed. The career of the great philanthropist, the Earl of Shaftesbury, is an impressive example of a child's so reacting to the failure of his parents as to build into the character an exceptional desire to serve others.

Sometimes the result of a child's being refused fellowship in his family leads him to creation of a fictitious child or adult who does give him the love that he craves. Thus imagination assumes the task of providing the relationship that the home has cruelly withheld. These substitutes, however, cannot fulfill the child's hunger for affection as can two parents, and may show themselves later in adult weaknesses.

Not only did Jesus draw from family experience terminology for the fundamental concepts of his gospel, but he also turned to the home for a great many of the illustrations that enabled him to clarify and voice his teachings. He chose commonplace events from the household routine as well as such dramatic episodes as that of the young man who left home, wasted his substance, finally awoke to his misdoings, and returned in humiliation to his father who welcomed him with open arms and celebrated his reformation by killing the fatted calf for a feast. The jealousy that this evoked in the other son and his protest that his good conduct had received no such recognition was again the sort of thing that not uncommonly appears in family relationships.

If one searches through the gospels for the references that are made by Jesus to the happenings that occur in home life, it becomes evident how greatly Jesus during his childhood was impressed by the events that attract the attention of the thoughtful child. It is apparent that Jesus responded to his domestic environment in accord with what we think of as being normal in a wholesome home. Indeed, his liberal choice of family experiences to make clear the meaning of his message indicates that nothing else in his early career was so impressive.

This fact is all the more significant because the

gospels reveal that he did not emotionally either anchor himself in the childhood period or so tie himself to his earthly parents that he could not achieve the independence necessary for the doing of his life work.

There came then his brethren and his mother, and, standing without, sent unto him calling him. And the multitude sat about him, and they said unto him, Behold, thy mother and thy brethren without seek for thee. And he answered them, saying, Who is my mother, or my brethren? And he looked round about on them which sat about him, and said, Behold my mother and my brethren! For whosoever shall do the will of God, the same is my brother, and my sister, and my mother.[1]

These words have had harsh interpretations as if they were a repudiation of home ties or a rebuke directed against his relatives for attempting to make home affection a rival of his mission. Such exegesis is a distortion of his teachings, a misapprehension through an exaggeration of the dramatic expression he made to bring out the necessity of his life's work having the right of way over every other interest. There is no suggestion that the members of his family were surprised by his attitude or would have chosen to have it otherwise. The declaration brings back the traditional story of his boyhood when his parents found him in the temple in the midst of the doctors, both hearing them and asking them questions, and he expressed surprise that they had not known where to seek him since he "had to be about His father's business." [2]

[1] Mark III: 31–35.
[2] Luke II: 49.

There is nothing to indicate that Jesus at any time repudiated his home, but he did make it clear that the way of life which he was advocating demanded an affection which transcended anything that appeared in family relationships, being all-compelling in quality and universal in range.

In the very brief record we have of the life of Jesus it is not strange that references to his boyhood and home life are so scanty. We have to assume that his experiences were those of the child in the better kind of Palestine Jewish households. We know that the typical Jewish home of the period was based on religion, that in accord with the ancestral tradition the father was priest of the home. The family maintained strong unity and discipline; the mother was given a respect and degree of equality that distinguished the Jewish practices from those of other eastern peoples. During the early years of the child, the mother was his teacher, then the task was taken over by the father. Later the child went outside the home for instruction in the law. His vocational training he received in association with his father.[3]

We cannot realize the full meaning of the strength of the Jewish family unless we take into account its political situation. Whenever a family carries on in isolation, whether it be on account of frontier conditions, as was true in our western country, or because of an alien environment, as has so many times proved true of first generation immigrants who in this coun-

---

[3] *History of Christianity in the Light of Modern Knowledge,* p. 133.

try found themselves segregated with people of their own kind, or as was true of the Jews because they existed as a conquered people, the significance of family relationship is intensified and the solidarity of the home greatly enhanced. To the Jewish people, sensitive to their loss of political sovereignty, the family offered privacy, independence, and self-respect. When they left their homes they might encounter contempt and persecution, but once they were back over their thresholds they were free and able to find in their ties of kinship a substitute for the normal self-expression denied them outside.

This strengthening of the family as a consequence of a more or less antagonistic social environment has continued through the centuries as the Jews have maintained themselves in the various countries as a people peculiar and apart. The family has been able to supply what to a greater or less degree has been socially and even politically denied due to the fact that the Jews have had for so long a time no nationality of their own. They could not proudly acclaim their national standing as did Paul at the time of Jesus when he said, "I am a Roman citizen," but they could find an even greater source of self-esteem in their knowledge of a family experience which in its strength of kinship has never been excelled.

Just as Jesus drew from family experience words to bring out the proper spirit of the Christian, so likewise he selected the word "father" as the best of all terms to suggest the proper relationship of man and God. None of his followers, when he taught them to pray, beginning, "Our Father who art in heaven," were likely to be misled and to think of this as an exact description, since the prerogatives of God were quite unlike those of the human head of the household. The similarity was in the meaning of the relationship; to portray that no other expression was so faithful and revealing as the word, "father." We cannot say that this concept of God was something entirely new, but certainly it became in the teachings of Jesus the central idea in his effort to drive home the proper relationship between man and God. The more common designations of the Old Testament seemed in contrast austere and distant. They emphasized fear and reverence, whereas his words, "My Father" or "Your Father," stressed affection, sympathy, understanding, and fellowship.

The fact that the faith of the Jews drew its spirit from the concepts and sentiments of the Old Testament shows how inevitable the collision was that finally led to the tragedy of the death of Jesus. The Old Testament is by no means destitute of intimations that point toward a relationship between God and man such as Jesus stressed, but the general current of thinking and feeling flowed in an opposite direction. The conflict between the orthodox religious leaders at the time of Jesus and himself was much more than that of different religious ideals. More fundamental were the divergent emotional attitudes, and nothing can measure the distance between them so clearly as the contrast of God as Jehovah and as our Father. This Jesus thoroughly understood but he also counted upon the domestic experience to help people see the higher quality of his interpretation of God. It was to be expected that he would have more response from those who were not by professional and social standing too greatly committed to the more conventional Jewish notions. The leaders had to break through a crust of habits, thought, and pride considerably thicker in their cases than was true of those of more humble homes who possibly found in their family relationships greater satisfactions and more revealing insights as to the meaning of human life.

Although Jesus drew from the domestic vocabulary his most descriptive terms, he did not make these suggestive symbols the exclusive means of interpreting his doctrine. Another favorite expression is "the Kingdom of God." This phrase had a familiar sound to his listeners because it seemed tied up with the teachings and prophecies of their sacred books. Its meaning, however, was not in the word, "kingdom," which carried over the notion of political supremacy, but in the totality of the conception which made the society he sought to establish distinctive not in power and political authority but in its distinguishing moral and spiritual qualities. To make this clear, the doctrine of the Kingdom of God had to be brought back into domestic experience for the uncovering of its meaning, thus the "Kingdom of God" became the "Kingdom of God our Father." This necessarily included the idea of brotherhood.

It quickly became evident that the Jewish people were tied to emotional expectations that made it difficult for them to accept the higher type of kingdom. They clung to the idea of kingdom because it promised the fulfillment of their hopes but they increasingly refused to reconstruct their thought of the nature of this kingdom and see it as a social order characterized by religious achievement in the spirit of an elevated domestic fellowship.

Again, we would expect those having prestige and holding positions of power to be less inclined to give up their hope of political resurrection. It was very human for them to cling to the idea of a reëstablished Jewish nation supported by the special concern of Jehovah. Since this was to bring them personal recognition and authority, it was the old familiar concept that promised fulfillment of their ambitions. The new teaching of Jesus—they were penetrating enough to see—must antagonize the prestige they already enjoyed since it would bring all the believers into a fellowship in which distinctions were ruled out. Since even the disciples closest to Jesus found it very difficult to accept this fact and had to be rebuked for their evidences of ambition, it is not strange that the well-established Jewish leaders clung so tenaciously to the idea of a kingdom on earth and were repelled by the contrary idea of a non-political brotherhood, based on motives that seemed to them characteristic of the family and impossible to extend to the general social relationships of persons not linked together by kinship.

To help his listeners break away from this deeply entrenched preconception of a political kingdom, Jesus found that the most promising idea of this radical reconstruction had to be drawn from domestic experience. In spite of Jesus' recourse to the familiar and impressive fellowship achieved within the home in his effort to give his disciples an understanding of what constituted his kingdom, tradition and desire caused his followers to hold to the idea of a triumphant, political dominance.

Jesus found himself contending with the human proneness to misconstrue ideas that are unpalatable and to replace them with others in accord with firmly entrenched emotional desires. This insistence upon changing one doctrine into its exact opposite, the theme of Dean Swift's *Tale of the Tub*, showed itself among the Jewish people in differing degrees of intensity, being strongest in the ruling class and least among the disciples. Even those he depended upon most, however, were not always free from this human weakness that frequently appears in the thinking of men and women and which was to prove itself in the history of Christianity the great tragedy of the faith. Undoubtedly, Jesus foresaw this. Indeed, it is believed by some that this was the deeper meaning of his struggle in the garden of Gethsemane. Jesus was forced to see that his words were to be quoted against his own teaching.

The Jewish unwillingness to accept a kingdom patterned after the family, because they coveted a reign of political triumph, was merely the first appearance of a spiritual perversion that again and again was to show itself in the history of the Christian church. This was, of course, nothing peculiar to his teaching.

Every leader who has made spiritual demands and gathered followers has found himself struggling with this same weakness of human nature. The higher the idealism, however, the more tragic appears its change into an opposite selfishness.

CHAPTER II

The Spiritual Function of the Family

SINCE this misconception persisted while Jesus was present in the flesh and able to rebuke ambitions absolutely contrary to his purposes, it is not strange that after his death his church struggled with the same temptation. The more usual meaning of "kingdom" was not only easier to grasp but provided motives to which selfish human nature was all too ready to respond. In contrast, the qualifying of the term, the very essence of his mission, made demands on character that could be successfully met only by those who, having caught his vision, had become thoroughly Christian and free from selfish expectations. That the spiritual emphasis was aggressively maintained by many and interpreted in the light of domestic experience is made clear by the description of the church as the Household of God. Again it was felt that the ideals forming the life philosophy that possessed the true follower were best described in a terminology that came from a relationship of common love. This choice was something more than a mere illustration, it was also a recognition and a tribute. Behind the usage, as was true in the teachings of Jesus, there was a realization that the family, when faithful to itself, led people to experiences that prepared them for the higher spiritual achievements of the Christian life.

In our everyday thinking and decisions, we are apt to take toward the family very nearly the same attitude that was in the minds of the Jews as they pondered the meaning of the kingdom. We regard the family from various angles, but because there is so much that it does that we do not ordinarily conceive of as essentially spiritual, we recognize its economic, social, educational, and child nurture functions, but are prone to forget that these are specific acts to meet immediate needs and that the essential significance of each of them is that it may become the means of bringing values into human life. Whatever form these services take, whatever purpose they fulfill, their underlying meaning is that they can encourage and support spiritual life. The mother, for example, does not need to be merely a skilled caretaking nurse. This ministration can also have a meaning for her, spiritualizing all she does, and her attitude naturally encourages a similar response in the child.

If we are not to think of the spiritual life as something outside our everyday experience, alien to the task we carry on, we have to recognize that the family, because it is charged with emotion and meaning, provides an exceptional opportunity for bringing the spiritual feeling into life and for using ordinary responsibilities for developing spiritual appreciation. The family can be a mere utility organization. It may faithfully carry on its functioning in such a way as to give no inkling of the potential meaning of the services it undertakes. This, however, need not happen, and when it does occur the family fails to achieve in the life of its members what should be supremely important.

Because of the latent meaning of the activities of the home, the reactions of its members bound together in the most intimate of associations, the family becomes potentially a spiritual ally of Christianity. The recognition Jesus gave the family from time to time, the use he made of its happenings, the ideas he drew from its fellowship, attest his realization of how especially close the wholesome family was to the social life he desired to establish on earth. His use of domestic illustration, his emphasis upon the deeper significance of family relationship, was not mere expediency; it was an effort to reveal the deeper meaning the home had in his own period. It was an acknowledgment of the natural alliance of the family and the Christian church.

This contribution of the family to the understanding of the message of Jesus continues to be true. Whenever the church surveys its resources it discovers that the family is its most significant ally. The state provides an authority and a means of quick action which the church, when it forgets the spiritual attainment promised through struggle and by slow progress, easily covets. Whenever the power of the state is enlisted to force people to assume Christian living, the consequences quickly reveal how limited and how dangerous this recourse to political authority always is in the attempt to advance the Christian way of life. On the contrary, the service of the family not only can be safely accepted, but without it the program of the church is seriously retarded. The reason for this is that the family by nature is essentially a spiritual relationship. It is not necessarily of the same spiritual quality as Christianity. Were it possible to reduce all the types of religious faith to a common spiritual denominator, even then it would be true that the spiritual meaning of domestic relationship is something different from that regarded as the common possession of the various religious attitudes toward life. The family therefore does not duplicate organized religion; nevertheless, in its functions it does lead toward a spiritual achievement which not only can prepare for religious experience but can be drawn within it.

The family also has an advantage over all other social institutions. It is the most mature in its evolution and the most thoroughly tied to elemental human needs, and it provides the most intimate of all relationships. No other institution is close enough in personal contacts to be trusted with the power that the home has over developing personalities. It is the meaningful associations of the family, the giving and responding in the spirit of love of its members, that protect the average home from the tyranny great authority tends to bring. Even in the early Roman family, where the power of the father was absolute, we may be sure that in practice the *patria potestas* [1] was restrained by the normal parental affection. The experiences of the Oneida Community are most impressive as they show us how

---

[1] Willystine Goodsell, *A History of Marriage and the Family*, pp. 117–118.

impossible it was by the most aggressive doctrinism to hold in check the parental impulses that safeguard a power lodged within the family.[2]

In the case of Christianity it is fair to say that its soundness at any moment of time can be discovered by its recognition of the spiritual significance of the family. If the church treats the family with indifference or looks upon the home as a rival, antagonistic because of its competition, it shows clearly a misinterpretation of its own mission. This, of course, does not mean that there are no individual families that on account of their unwholesomeness conflict with Christianity and hamper its progress. No true appraisal of modern life leads to doubt regarding this. The trouble comes not because there are detrimental traits, hiding in the family, that make family life *per se* an enemy of Christian character, but because the whole purpose of the family in such instances is not fulfilled. Such families may be strong through external pressure, functioning as an enterprise of necessity, but they lack through retardation their most distinctive substance, the realization of spiritual fellowship.

It is easy for those who think of spiritual experience as an accretion added on to ordinary life activities, rather than as a spirit permeating them, to fail to see the inherent spiritual possibilities of family associations. Such persons rob spiritual experience of its vitality by seeking to find it in the ecstatic. They cannot realize that it can transfigure ordinary lives, but hunt for it in occult, magical happenings that to them

[2] Pierrepont Noyes, *My Father's House*, p. 67.

are spiritually genuine only when removed from the mundane world. Nothing could be more contrary to the teachings of Jesus.

The family is the greatest distance possible from such misinterpretations of Christian experience. What the home does ties it closely to the everyday world. It gathers its spiritual significance not from discovering how to escape from everyday human interests but by lifting these to a higher level of significance as they become the means of expressing extraordinary affection, loyalty and unselfishness.

This support which the family normally gives to the Christian program is true for all three major interests that the family includes. These are marriage, sex, and parenthood. Each has at times been regarded as essentially unspiritual, a source of antagonizing motivations. In the order of the attack that they have encountered from church leadership we find sex most frequently indicted, and parenthood least of all. The Shakers, however, remind us that even parenthood has been interpreted as fundamentally evil, even though there could be no denial that a spiritual program that excluded the bringing of children into the world would mean the elimination of the human race. It was felt that human survival would be well taken care of through the unspiritual outlook of those who clung to parenthood in spite of its essential evil.

The moral and spiritual opportunities of parenthood are to most persons so obvious that any program for life that denies them seems a social monstrosity. It is not enough, however, if we are to have a true picture of the spiritual meaning of the family, to realize the potential contributions to character that come from the intimate affection and fellowship of parent and child. There is need of a more analytic discernment, an understanding in some detail of the interchange of influence of child and parent.

The parent is, under normal circumstances, so closely knit to the life of the infant as to make him almost an extension of the parent's personality. However hazardous this may prove through lack of self-discipline or insight, it does give the basis for a transference of interest away from one's self that is unexcelled as a source of sympathy, and only duplicated by the husband-wife relationship. The helplessness of the child adds, however, a feeling of responsibility that is not present in the usual husband-wife comradeship. The parent is tied to the child, but at the same time is forced to recognize the developing of what so quickly becomes another personality. He has to see this coming forth from the endowment that the child possesses and which immediately begins to unfold through the growth process which the parent observes. As this goes on day by day, the parent can hardly escape seeing that he is helping to create another life, nor can he, unless made obtuse through self-conceit, fail to realize how independently this life is forming itself.

The parent who becomes aware of this double process, a ministration that may direct but cannot control the forming of another human life, is by the experience led to see and feel profoundly the potential values of the earthly existence, an insight which makes spiritualizing possible. Life becomes pregnant with meeting, a challenge to character.

The child likewise enters upon an increasing realization of the meaning of the world in which he is placed, through the medium of his mother's and father's interest in him. Their discovery of values influences his capacity to find in life spiritual significance, and this in time gives him the beginning of a spiritual career. The naturalness of this, the need of permitting him to have his own characteristic reactions, was never more impressively brought out than by Bishop Phillips Brooks' famous sermon on the religion of the child.

Christianity's struggle with asceticism had a greater meaning than appears on the surface. It involved decisions as to the meaning of the Christian way of life and, therefore, brought forth a fundamental issue. Asceticism could not remain merely a protest against earthly interests or an attempt to live a life free from one of nature's most aggressive impulses, since it had to be justified by an interpretation of the obligations or at least ideals that face the followers of Jesus. Its advocates encountered a stubborn fact imposed by nature, and convincing defense had to be given for any program that attempted to circumvent this edict that human survival and family life could come only through sexual relations of male and female. Sex and reproduction do not demand the family, but, on the other hand, the family tends to disappear in the proportion that asceticism removes sex and reproduction from human experiences.

There were two historic happenings at the beginning of Christianity that naturally encouraged the ascetic emphasis that religious zeal so often invites. Jesus, the founder of the faith, had remained unmarried and Paul, who chiefly took over his leadership, followed his example. In neither case was there good reason for regarding this choice as an acceptance of the ascetic philosophy of life. The career of Jesus was not one that rightly included marriage and the establishment of a family. Judging his decision merely as a test of ordinary human prudence, it would have been unethical for him to have married and established a family. His divine purpose made his program imperative.

The situation was nearly the same in the case of Paul. His roving life, persecution, and commitment to a responsibility that allowed no opportunity for domestic obligations meant that his marrying would have been evidence of selfishness, creating a rival to his chosen purpose in life. In his case, as we shall see, his influence went beyond being an example since he regarded the choice he had to make as the most desirable one for his unmarried Christian followers.

Neither Jesus nor Paul, however, countenanced any teaching that struck against the wholesomeness of the family. They directed no assault upon sex or reproduction. On the contrary Jesus, by his presence at the wedding at Cana, gave recognition and approval of marriage and even Paul regarded it under certain circumstances as expedient. Although we, looking back, not entangled by the circumstances that confronted the Christians during the first century, can see that there was no doctrinal significance in the not marrying of Jesus and Paul, the implication of this choice of the founder and the great missionary of the faith was to encourage the ascetic trend in the first followers. Moreover, the same condition that confronted St. Paul influenced others prominent in the church to follow his example and remain unmarried. An expediency during one period easily became an ideal later for Christian leaders whose circumstances radically differed from those of Paul.

There was a compromise position that avoided the extreme of thoroughgoing asceticism. This looked upon sex merely as a function of reproduction and, therefore, regarded intercourse as proper only for the purpose of bringing children into the world and establishing a family. This attempt to restrict sex to its reproductive purpose is familiar to us because, as a theory at least, it has had considerable vogue even in our time. Sex is debased except as it functions biologically as the necessary means for bringing forth offspring. The difficulty with this attitude was and is that human development has carried sex beyond the stage of expression characteristic of lower animals. Evolution has lifted us above the dominance of the instinct which is nature's provision on the lower level for the ongoing of life. Human sex has taken on in great measure emotional and psychic characteristics, and this accretion runs counter to any interpretation of sex that restricts it to reproduction. It is not merely that such an effort strikes against the human desire to make the most of the pleasurable aspect of sex relations. It also denies sex the opportunity to become a part of the affectionate spiritual fellowship of husband and wife, an achievement of relationship inconsistent with the idea that sex has among humans no other purpose than the propagating of the race.

The full meaning of this inconsistency we discover through the experience of the normal young man and woman who attempt to maintain a sex policy that justifies their intimacy only as a means of reproduction. Their program drives them into continuous struggle, one that invites the hazards of various forms of perversion, nervous strain, ending perchance in the woman's becoming frigid or the man's becoming impotent. The program leans toward asceticism because it regards sex as something animal and non-spiritual, to be tolerated merely because it is a necessity for biological survival. Such a position cannot but discolor normal domestic relationship. Not only does it create stress which demonstrates that human sex has put itself beyond the confines of an instinct tied to a temporary erotic season, but it also strikes at the comradeship of husband and wife, which naturally includes sex relations as an expression of affection.

Those who have inclinations toward asceticism but cannot convince themselves of the reasonableness of an absolute repudiation of sex find this policy of restricting sex to reproduction an agreeable compromise.

They fail to see that they are attempting to struggle against the human development of sex, the enrichment that permits it to be a distinctive expression of love, far removed from any merely reproductive mechanism. Even when Christian teaching has escaped a thorough-going asceticism, it has frequently supported this milder insistence that sex be accepted only as a necessary condition for the ongoing of the race. Christian leadership sometimes feared the pleasurable aspects of sex as a potential rival to the commitment needed for spiritual living. Teachings that tolerated sex as a necessary evil but refused to accept it as a means of grace appeared from time to time, and, even when not much accepted by the majority of believers, considerably hampered any recognition of the possible contribution of sex to a fellowship of love and spiritual growth.

The interpretation the famous Swiss psychiatrist, Jung, gave of the libido helps us to understand the potential spiritual significance of sex. The libido, according to Jung and in contrast with the teaching of Freud, represented an all-inclusive but differentiated psychic energy which found its outlet in multitudinous human interests and activities. It is the desire drive, the pressure of craving that moves each of us to transform inner, nervous force into outer behavior. He regarded it as a fundamental inclination, essentially spiritual. It therefore antagonized any non-spiritual sexual tendency or conflict. If the sex life remains primitive, it is retarded, failing to take on qualities that belong to its normal development. The conflicts so frequently found in the feeling, thinking and acting in the field of sex are the consequences, not of a basic antagonism between sex and culture, but of a failure which came from an imperfect development of the libido.

Whatever may be our attitude toward this philosophic interpretation of the sex impulse, there is abundant basis for insisting upon this elaboration of the sexual impulse which gives it spiritual meaning. We constantly have to recognize the great distance there is between animal passion and a mature sex adjustment. It is common for people to use the words, "passion" and "love," in order to bring out the distinction between two different levels of achievement in the sexual life. The addition which distinguishes one from the other is to be found in the meaning associated with the sex act. In one case it is primitive, meager, and instinctive; in the other it is complex, mature, full of content and replete with emotional meaning. It is this variable accumulation of values which constitutes the human sex problem and which necessarily increases its significance with the evolution of culture and the development of maturity in the individual.

The difficulties our young people have in achieving good sexual adjustment, especially at the beginning of marriage, give evidence of the present significance of this non-physical aspect of sex. The most common maladjustments are caused by psychic or social influences, even though the form the trouble takes is physical. Nothing could more clearly show how distant normal human sex life is from the automatic passion which operates according to season in the life of the animal. It is this accretion that sex has gathered during human evolution that makes possible its spiritual meaning.

The relationship of male and female, even in common thinking, is recognized as meager unless there be in addition to the primitive, that is, the physical sex attraction, a personal response which at least is an elemental expression of regard even if it cannot be accredited with being genuine affection. When this emotional quality is absent, the deficiency is so great as to justify our describing the relationship as abnormal, even though from a purely body point of view the relationship can be said to be satisfactory.

A great deal of the damage that has come to the individual's sex adjustment through unwholesome conditioning has resulted from older people interpreting sex to the child as it appears on the level of primitive passion, thus giving a false impression of normal human experience. This erroneous attitude toward sex has made it difficult for the individual to discover the true significance of the comradeship of husband and wife.

Christianity, of course, is not the only religion that had to struggle with ascetic trends. The religious thinking and practices even of primitive people reveal how easily human nature can be captivated by ecstatic emotionalism and thereby led to crusade against the sexual impulse. These assaults take every conceivable expression. We are, therefore, not justified in thinking that Christianity's struggle with asceticism was a religious peculiarity. Our interest, however, is not in tracing the psychic trend that has appeared so frequently in human history as to seem a characteristic perversion of normal endowment, but rather in seeing the working of this within the Christian church. Since this development of asceticism has antagonized one of the essential components of family life, it must be dealt with in any attempt to analyze the relationship of Christianity to the family and, because of its importance, deserves being made a chapter by itself.

CHAPTER III

Christianity and Sex

IT IS easy to understand why there has been such suspicion of sex on the part of the church leadership. The sex impulse, because of its roots in body life, can most easily be detached from the domestic complex and then made the means of exploiting one's self as well as others. This hazard, although it justifies warning and discipline, does not support the idea that sex is necessarily a source of spiritual conflict. If sex were inevitably the cause of such conflict, Christianity would be forced toward asceticism and could never honestly regard the family as an ally.

The historic development of Christian doctrine shows us that this feeling that sex constituted a foreign element, hostile to spiritual achievement, has found expression again and again. Indeed, the shadow of asceticism still continues. Looking backward we get glimpses of the way the teachings of the historic church were deflected and through their own unsoundness have struck at an inevitable element in family experience. The logic of the domestic situation is unmistakable. If sex by its nature is antagonistic to the spiritual experiences that are possible within the family, it remains a necessary but alien element and deserves the suspicion of Christian leadership.

There is considerable literature dealing with the influence of the sex impulse on religion. Some theorists have gone so far as to insist that religion in itself is a derivative of human eroticism. It would be strange indeed if so fundamental an aspect of human nature was left outside the life attitude that seeks both to dominate and spiritualize every aspect of behavior. Nevertheless, we find in Christianity, just as we do in other religions, the attempt to barricade personality against sex, even though the effort may disclose curious inconsistencies. The ascetic traditions of Christianity need to be reckoned with because they repudiate the idea that sex can be incorporated in the domestic complex as a necessary and legitimate element and a potential source of spiritualizing fellowship between a man and woman. The obvious fact that many individuals in their life experience fail to find anything in sex that carries beyond the body satisfaction and that they do find difficulty in maintaining a balance that prevents a shift toward either the exaggeration of sex or its attempted suppression, reveals the origin of the protest appearing in Christian doctrine or policy in the form of a militant asceticism.

There is evidence in the austere habits of the early Christians, and especially in their fasting, that the appetite for food also met with restraint. If there had been associated with food the psychic complications and the social consequences belonging to sex, it would surely have encountered the same aggressive protest.

Sex, therefore, was not the only expression of this desire of the early believers to reduce to the least possible proportion any body demand that, because of its impetuosity, appeared hazardous to a concentration on spiritual affairs. However, because of its characteristics, sex invited the ascetic attitude more than any of the other primitive appetites.

We cannot put ourselves in the place of the early followers of Christ who leaned toward asceticism, and realize how they felt, unless we see that recognition of the sexual impulse interfered with their concentrating upon a way of life that separated them from earthly interests. Sex also, at least in the male, insists upon its own concentration. The impulse cannot function unless it crowds out, for the moment, all other matters. This fact made it seem more of a rival than any of the other body appetites. One can eat indifferently with his thoughts elsewhere even to such an extent that he cannot later recall the food he swallowed. This lack of attention to eating commonly happens in the rush of urban life. A woman can outwardly go through a similar disregard of her part in sexual intercourse even if this robs her of the value of the experience, making it similar to that of the professional prostitute. This unconcern, however, is not open to the male, since to attempt it quickly checks his potency. Since the directing of the Christian program was chiefly in the hands of men, it was natural that the doctrine and the practices of the church should reflect at times a masculine protest against what seemed to be an encroachment of sex upon the greater purpose of life.

We have no reason to suppose that sex, even in the life of those possessing spiritual passion, could always be easily suppressed. Indeed, we have the testimony found in the writings of the Church Fathers, that the acceptance of the ascetic program frequently brought conflict. So far as this did occur, the Christian who had resigned himself to the minimizing of sex would have all the more reason to suspect and feel that it constituted an intrusion upon the self-chosen religious commitment, an assault that must be given no quarter. Thus the policy of asceticism would, because of the emotional struggle it brought about, make sex seem all the more an alien impulse that should be regarded as an enemy of the faith.

In such an atmosphere of antagonism to sex there was no hope of recognizing its fulfillment-purpose. At this point, modern science has brought a great change. Since the latter part of the nineteenth century there has been, at least among thinkers, some slight realization of the physiological and nervous significance of sex. We have come to appreciate that it offers relaxation and creative vitality that give it a value aside from its relation to reproduction. It is probably an overstatement to insist that this was entirely a modern discovery. Even in our own time a multitude of persons who have no knowledge of the findings of medical and psychiatric sciences know through personal experience that the sexual function contributes to the body well-being. This, doubtless, has always been true since man began to be reflective, and this understanding did not need to wait until the coming of critical thinking and investigation. Those, however, who were responsible for the leadership of the early church did not need to take into account in their preachment the newer insight regarding the physical values of good sexual adjustment, which only recently have received just recognition even by physicians and psychiatrists.

Early Christianity was not seeking to build a program for a well-balanced physical and mental career. It was in deadly conflict with a hostility that struck at it from every side. Its chief task was to survive and to spread itself into every part of the known world. Its spirit had to be missionary. It was certain to be smothered out unless it could keep its distinction and not only protect itself from pagan civilization, but permeate Rome with its spirit, and thus convert and conquer those who sought its destruction. The church had no choice but to crusade, and any deflecting influence, from whatsoever source it came, could only be regarded as a danger. Movements that encounter terrific competition bring forth a leadership that has neither the time nor the disposition to weigh their message with discrimination. Instead, their only hope of success comes from a driving power that carries them toward their purpose, indifferent or hostile to anything that seems trivial, distracting or incompatible. It has frequently been said by the Christian ministry that when the church is at peace, then it is in peril.

We who live in the better days which Christianity, through its struggle, largely has made possible, are in no position to feel the intensity of the religious passion that characterized those who in the early centuries followed Jesus amid contrary social conditions. We, therefore, are too likely to pass judgment upon the ascetic trends that were, from time to time, uncovered in the early church, as if these had the same meaning that they would have if they appeared in our own time. Because of this same failure to distinguish between the differing social situations, the believer in our day may look backward and find, in the historic occurrences of asceticism, support for a life program that is essentially morbid. This, however, cannot happen unless there is failure to discover the positive value of wholesome family adjustment which in our time, from necessity, includes the sexual adjustment of the husband and the wife.

False interpretation of the meaning of the family has to precede the resurrection on religious grounds of the asceticism that attempts to throttle sex. Since this erroneous view of a basic human relationship, detrimental to the building of successful family life, may come from any effort to revive the ascetic attitude, there is need for the Christian of today thoroughly to understand the background of its expression as it occurred in the early Christian Church.

Disciples are always tempted to imitate the externals of the life of the leader whom they follow. Those who enlist in religious movements seem especially liable to this emphasis upon what is external and minor as compared with the basic spiritual significance of their leader's career. Among the early Christians this disposition naturally tended to stress the ascetic aspects of the life of Jesus. It cannot be justly said that they tried to substitute one for the other but rather that they tended to magnify conditions which, although associated with the mission of Jesus in his effort to establish the Kingdom of God amid the circumstances in which he had to work, were nevertheless a temporary scaffolding in comparison with the spiritual way of life that he was trying to build.

What we now need to remember is the resistance that this trend met with which prevented the church from drifting into such an outlook upon life as was illustrated by the Essenes. The disposition to coerce an impulse regarded as base and treacherous is always stimulated and shaped by the historic conditions found in a definite place and period. This is well illustrated by the asceticism that appeared early in the history of the Christian church. Although the influences that led to the ascetic trend were many, as is always true in any pronounced social reaction, we can now detect four that show us how the repudiation of sex as a portion of domestic fellowship occurred. These were (1) moral and social conditions within the Roman Empire, (2) the example and teachings of St. Paul, (3) introvertive protest against the sex impulse, and (4) sex being made the symbol of the worldly life which the Christian must renounce.

It is always difficult to make just appraisal of the social and moral conditions of any distant historic period. This is especially true when we seek to picture the situation that confronted the early Christian. We have a limited literature from which to draw our information, and even these writings reveal bias and chiefly reflect the life of the wealthy, politically dominating class of society. It is recognized by historians that descriptions of Roman social life based upon the writings that have come down to us, chiefly from the first century and from the early part of the second century, represent only the people of wealth and prominence; and that the statements of the Church Fathers, who especially reacted to the vice and corruption of their time, have led to an exaggeration of the evils existing in the Roman Empire during the early development of Christianity. This sensational emphasis upon the darkest side of Roman conditions, of which the writings of Pliny the Younger are an example, hampers the attempt to draw a faithful picture of a civilization that has passed. Even, however, when we allow for exaggeration, there can be no doubt that the life of the Roman people revealed a moral decline. This does not mean that the social degeneration was consistent, but rather that there was clear evidence of cruelty, vice and corruption.

It is not difficult to draw from the source of our knowledge facts, statements, and sentiments that give us a picture of a vicious social environment, both contrary to the Christian way of life and uncompromisingly hostile. The Church Fathers do not give us a false perspective, if we keep in mind that conditions were not consistently evil and that Christian interpreters were in no mood or position to furnish us with an unprejudiced account of Roman life. The great number of slaves, even if their treatment was not gen-

erally as cruel as we might think from the reports that
have come down from happenings on large estates, the
increase of luxury, the rapid expansion of Roman rule,
the concentration of power at the capital city, the
inhuman gladiatorial shows, the licentiousness and the
decaying of domestic values, especially in the wealthy
and leading families, forced the church for its own
survival to maintain a program of separation. The
persecutions that from time to time were carried on
by the government intensified this effort of Christians
to barricade themselves from the many evils that confronted them from every side.

Every Christian was eager to keep himself unspotted
from the world. As is always true in a period of moral
confusion, sex stood out as the foremost expression of
the existing depravity. The conditions were not con-
ducive to a balanced attitude and, as was to be expected, the moral recoil of the Christian tended toward
an asceticism that was both protective and was also a
means of emotional compensation. However fortunate
this reaction was for the survival of the church, placed
in an alien environment, it necessarily proved trouble-
some for Christians of a later time living under different circumstances, by making it appear that a complete
adherence to ascetic practices was an obligation for all
followers of Jesus.

St. Paul in his writings several times gave expression
to ideas that encouraged the trend toward making
asceticism an ideal of the Christian. The most conse-
quential of these ideas had to do with marriage. If we
place ourselves in the position of Paul and accept his

convictions, his counsels accord with sound judgment.
He was certainly influenced in part by his belief that
the end of the existing world was near and the second
coming of Christ at hand. Therefore, it was no time
for the believers to start new families. Even, however,
had he not held to this conviction, at least during the
early period of his missionary career, the situation in
which Christians found themselves, the ominous future
that appeared to face them, would have led any person
of good sense to discourage the founding of a family
and the bringing of children into the world. He doubtless foresaw even more aggressive persecution and
realized what this could mean in homes with young
children.

If one asks, how then did Paul expect Christianity
to survive and expand?—the answer is, through con-
version. This, of course, brought hazard to many
homes that were likely to suffer through the sentence
to death of one or both parents. But to accept a situation already existing was quite different from encouraging new marriages and the starting of new
homes. Even so, Paul's advice to his young followers
not to marry was conditional, as shown by his statement:

> But I say to the unmarried and to widows, It is good
> for them if they abide even as I. But if they have not
> continency, let them marry: for it is better to marry than
> to burn.[1]

It seems questionable whether these words deserve
the harsh interpretation they have in recent years gen-

---

[1] First Corinthians VII: 8, 9.

erally received. When the situation of Christians was so precarious, justifying, as he saw it, abstinence from marriage for reasons of prudence, his words showed his recognition of the fact that even at such a time it might be wiser for some individuals to marry than to carry on the fierce struggles that would mark their keeping to the single life. He did not intend to have later Christians read into his words, "Marriage is for Christians always undesirable and only to be entered upon because it is better than being consumed by passion." He was not dealing with a theory but was confronted with a social situation that needed realistic counsel. Who of us, placed in similar social conditions and responsible for influencing the welfare of others, would not wish to discourage marrying, although realizing that even in such unstable circumstances marrying might mean for some a better choice than remaining single.

Whatever Paul may have meant by his words, it is well for us to remember that love as well as passion can be a consuming flame. Paul shows unusual tolerance in his position regarding marriage in suggesting that he is stating personal opinions and does not want his words taken as a command. It is not strange, however, that they carried over with an authority that made them in later time a source of support of the ascetic way of life, influencing the feeling that marriage was an inferior choice, and retarding the advance in the status of women. Paul could not be effective in his own time without running the risk of being used later as a means of obstructing the ongoings of the spiritual progress of the Christian church. Words lifted out of their historical background can become as misinterpretive of the spirit of their author as phrases and sentences dislodged from their context.

In spite of his conviction that the second coming of Jesus was near, and his realization of the hazards facing the Christian believers which meant that those who married had little hope of domestic stability, St. Paul did not insist that marriage should be denied those professing the Christian faith but he did believe that those who kept single made the wiser choice. He also feared that the distractions sure to follow any attempt to build family life would be likely to lessen the zeal of Christians, who should be thoroughly given up to the advancing of the kingdom. So far as he personally was concerned, the impulse of sex, even the affection that led toward marriage, could hardly seem any other than a distraction, insignificant as compared with the missionary opportunity of the Christ-led followers. In writing to the Corinthians he made his position clear in the following words:

So then both he that giveth his own virgin *daughter* in marriage doeth well; and he that giveth her not in marriage shall do better. A wife is bound for so long time as her husband liveth; but if the husband be dead, she is free to be married to whom she will; only in the Lord. But she is happier if she abide as she is, after my judgment (sic): and I think that I also have the Spirit of God.[2]

The introvertive appeal made by Christianity brought into the fellowship individuals who were in-

---

[2] First Corinthians VII: 38–40.

clined toward an ascetic protest against the demands of the sex impulse. Although the Christian church by its teachings through the centuries has kept a good balance of introvertive and extravertive interests, at times and by certain groups one of these opposite outlooks upon life has been magnified at the expense of the other. Introvertive experience is an absolute necessity in any creative period of religion. In order to have a basis for personal conviction of the realities of spiritual experience, the individual must discover and maintain an inner life which gives him values independent of the external evironment. Historic Christianity tempered this by an insistence that true emotionalism, inner-life experience, does not exhaust itself in mystic, self-contained emotionalism, but finds an outlet in Christlike ministrations. Sound faith led to good works. Jesus' insistence upon the superiority of introvertive value in his rebuke of Martha discloses an imperative of experience for those entering into the meaning of his Kingdom of God. The core of Paul's teachings, that faith was the essential Christian possession and the source of Christlike practices, is another illustration of the introvertive emphasis.

The introvertive program has its hazards just as does the extravertive. The desire to maintain inward command easily leads to an exaggeration of the struggle against any pressure that appears in the life as an external force. Sex, by its compelling attraction, seems to shift the center from inner values to outer values and therefore is interpreted as something that should be resisted. The fact that there is an inner welcoming of this environmental assault is regarded as a patriotic citizen looks upon the fifth columnist who opens his arms to the invading army. Paul's description of the struggle within him between flesh and spirit invited the distortion that found its climax in the doctrine of virginity. Thus the Christian doctrine lined up with the Hellenistic mysticism of Platonic origin and repudiated the biblical idea of creation, thereby undermining domestic idealism.

The sexual impulse, because it demands a partner, forces peculiar recognition of social dependence. The fulfillment of one's own desires requires sharing the experience with one's mate. Introversion, as it moves far from the center, balks at this idea of looking to another person for one's own self-fulfillment. The early Christian who had any inclination toward this reaction was encouraged by his social situation. To a great extent his environment appeared hostile. His refuge was in his fellowship with God. He became suspicious of any desire that drew him away from his mystic concentration. Instead, he was eager to show not only freedom from, but contempt of, the affairs of the world that meant so much to those who did not share his experience of life with God. Thus the Christian was tempted to use the earthly existence with its appetites, passions and needs, as background to demonstrate his release from the motives that move ordinary men. Naturally sex became his favorite choice for illustrating his removal from the world in which most non-Christians had to seek their values.

These men and women who had utterly given themselves to a life with God were not content merely to practice their convictions but in their preachment insisted that their way of life was the only genuine Christian experience. Paul's letters, with their criticisms and rebukes, show us that there were a considerable number of his followers in the various churches who were a long distance from being unspotted by the world. Their failure, as his exhortations reveal, frequently showed itself along lines of sex. Such occurrences could only increase the feeling of those who saw in sex the most tempting impulse of the body, the one that chiefly distracted from the inner life and attempted to rival its values. St. Paul saw in marriage a way of escape for those who were not strong enough to follow his example but, although he admitted that this course was open to Christian youth, his words frankly carried a suggestion that those who entered matrimony were driven from the superior manner of life by insufficient self-control.

Finally sex became the symbol of the worldly values that the Christian needed to sacrifice. Of all the earthly impulses it was the one that could most safely be denied. Food-taking could be reduced to a minimum but unless fasting was carried out with some discretion it became suicide. The Christian could deny himself sleep and rest but here also his control of the body was limited. Sex was a physical demand of a different order. It was as strong, or at least could become as strong, as the others but, even so, it could be denied expression without seeming to hurt the body or destroy health. Repudiation is always easier than adjustment. The one requires the discrimination and discipline that go with insight, while the other demands only a stubborn, uncompromising self-denial. The one requires learning to make intelligent use of a human endowment; the other demands only the persistence of a hostile emotion. Since there is always potentially present in any captivating enterprise the enticement to prove the strength and sincerity of one's commitment by doing something hard, the sex impulse, because of its force, is apt to be the first choice for the test of sacrifice.

Sex was regarded as mere body pleasure. Reproduction was different, and even here the necessary sexual prelude, because it brought body satisfactions, led to the feeling that it was something that could only be approved because without it human survival became impossible. There was no recognition of the organic value of sex experience. This lack of appreciation was not strange when we realize that the physiological benefits of sex even yet are only faintly realized by most people. Sex is still regarded as either a means of pleasure or a means of perpetuating the race. Even medical science has been slow to appreciate the nervous and organic contributions of sex and reproduction. It was the theories of Sigmund Freud that led science to investigate sex seriously and to seek knowledge of its nervous and psychic meaning and influence. The discoveries of endocrinology also forced new attitudes toward the sex equipment of the body.

The consequence of these changes is that our feeling

toward the sexual endowment has grown more and more different from that which led the early Christians toward their ascetic attitude. There is increasing recognition within the church of the need of more effective counseling in order that there may be fewer problems of physical incomptability between husbands and wives. This is not primarily an effort to increase body pleasure for its own sake, but rather a practical attempt to help the sex impulse to function normally in marriage because this strengthens love and enhances personality.

The Christian doctrine of sin influenced asceticism because sex was regarded as a chief source of human temptation. Indeed, it came to be the basic explanation of evil. This was dramatized in the fall of Eve. Not only was she held responsible for the coming of sin into the world, but she was made representative so that every woman partook of her evil.

This philosophizing seems to many of us now clearly a masculine protest against the struggle of those who sought to coerce normal human impulse in their effort to maintain the ascetic program. The desire of the Christian to free himself from earthly entanglements expressed itself in an attitude toward sex which made it the center of conflict. Among the sacrifices that the true Christian was expected to make, sexual impulse frequently stood first because it, more than any other body craving, could be made a symbol of worldliness.

The fall, the consequence of the evil-doing of Eve, destroyed the naturalness of spiritual experience. The better life had to be achieved through struggle. It was not a normal growth of persons seeking the good life, but something that came from the repudiation of natural impulses, the taking on of non-earthly purposes, and the committing of one's self to the task of conquering the world for Christ, in the spirit of a pilgrim who looked for a "city which hath the foundations, whose builder and maker is God." [3]

The natural consequence of this thinking was the development of the idea that virginity was the best possible proof of a Christian's being divorced from the world. If we are justified in accepting *The Acts of Paul and Thekla* as a means of insight as to how Christians of the first and second century interpreted Paul's attitude toward virginity, we have in the following words a good illustration of the way in which virginity became evidence of the Christian's disregard of earthly interests:

Blessed are they that keep themselves chaste, because they shall be called the temples of God. Blessed are the souls and bodies of virgins, for they shall be pleasing to God, and shall not lose the reward of their chastity. Blessed are they that despise the world, for they shall be pleasing to God. [4]

In any discussion of asceticism it is necessary to keep in mind how easily the sex impulse can be turned from its normal expression. This is something that we now understand better than did they who were without the advantage of recent science, but only those who

---

[3] Hebrews XI: 10.
[4] *Acts of Paul and Thekla*, 4, p. 63, quoted by F. C. Conybeare, *Monuments of Early Christianity*.

have had special contact with the deviations of sex, or who are acquainted with the growing literature concerned with this problem, can appreciate the sensitiveness of the impulse to environmental influences. This is especially true in early childhood, although it is doubtful whether childhood experiences have the determining influence assumed by some of the extreme interpreters of sex conditioning. The probability is that we have a tendency to read meaning into childhood experiences, and to forget that in most instances acquired perversion comes from an accumulation and is not merely the outcoming of one particular occurrence or suggestion.

The keenest imagination cannot picture the wide range of sexual aberration as the counselor discovers it. In addition to the glaring departures from what is generally regarded as normal, we have a great quantity of minor, inconsequential idiosyncrasies that can be catalogued as fetishes. All these variations, both those that are extreme and those that are moderate, according to the generally accepted standards, reveal how open sex impulse is to social conditioning.

We commonly have reactions of disgust, guilt, fear, and shame that become associated with sex desire. They can reshape or inhibit one of the strongest impulses the human body possesses. It is, therefore, not strange that in the early centuries of Christianity sex was frequently turned toward some form of asceticism. This development cannot be used as evidence of the weakening of the impulse. On the contrary, the careers of those whose sex life becomes abnormal teach us that the very strength of the ascetic attitude is at times the outcropping of excessive sexuality, so that the aggressiveness of the impulse becomes a source of the coercion that keeps it under cover or forces it to take a morbid coloring. If, therefore, the early Christian found himself in conflict with a physical passion that he was determined to suppress, this experience would increase his attack on the impulse, thus encouraging the ascetic program for life.

There has been a disposition among Protestants to regard asceticism as a special liability of the Catholic church. This was voiced by Lecky as follows:

Such is the ideal of Protestantism. No one can deny that it is a lofty one or that it has borne good fruit. "Protestant and industrial civilization," says Lecky, "has tended to elevate the virtues of good humour, frankness, active courage, sanguine energy, buoyancy of temper," and to "deprecate the ideal type of Catholicism," which is "feeble and effeminate." This is certainly far apart from that other ideal. There the strong humanness which seems so good is counted a thing to be conquered. The flesh is to be subdued by fasting. Personality is to be extinguished in unquestioning obedience. The great impulse of sexual love, the impulse which fills the spring with song and the summer with the scent of flowers, which casts the romantic glow men never weary of across the commonplace of human life, is to be annihilated in virginity.

Protestants have not merely rejected the ascetic ideal of life. They have failed to understand it. They have very often hated it, and almost always dreaded it.[5]

---

[5] James O. Hannay, *The Spirit and Origin of Christian Monasticism*, pp. 6–7.

This distinction does not seem justified by the facts. Any comparison between the two branches of Christianity, to be fair, must, of course, take into account only what has occurred since the days of Luther. From that time the ascetic trend has appeared both in Catholic and Protestant preachments and practices. The difference is, however, that the Catholic church has recognized the naturalness of sex and has provided within its system the means for its expression. On the other hand, Protestant asceticism has generally been carried on as a crusade. It has either provided the core of a denominational grouping, as it did for the Shakers, or it has been a rallying ideal within a group, as has been true, for example, of some who held to the doctrine of perfection. In this latter case, the movement has had to justify itself in claiming a superiority, by insisting that the road that had been chosen was the only one for the genuine followers of Jesus.

It cannot rightly be said that asceticism is the ideal of the Catholic church. It is not regarded as a universal obligation. It is an acceptable way of life, one that can be thought of as especially worthy because it is difficult and represents an unrivaled commitment. Even so, it is not, as asceticism is likely to be in a Protestant crusade, a duty of all Christians. If Catholic doctrine were to take this turn, it would come into collision with the teaching of the church, that marriage is a sacrament. This belief that matrimony becomes a source of sanctifying grace checks an ascetic crusade, such as has at times vexed Protestantism. The doctrine of sacramental grace was stated by Pius XI in part as follows:

They [the faithful] open up for themselves [through the sacrament] a treasure of sacramental grace from which they draw supernatural power for the fulfilling of their rights and duties faithfully, holily, perseveringly even unto death. Hence this Sacrament not only increases sanctifying grace, the permanent principle of the supernatural life, in those who, as the expression is, place no obstacle [obex] in its way, but also adds particular gifts, dispositions, seeds of grace by elevating and perfecting the natural powers.[6]

Whatever arguments may be urged against celibacy, they cannot be used to demonstrate that the Catholic church is committed to asceticism. We Protestants are not willing to consider Jesus an ascetic because he did not marry. We would also protest against any insistence that men like Bishop Phillips Brooks, who remained unmarried, were, because of this, committed to asceticism. Although we do not like the idea of the clergy being denied marriage, we are familiar with the religious leader who prefers not to marry. We recognize in his choice, as it influences his Christian services, both advantages and disadvantages. The Catholics believe that this refraining from marriage is a duty because the priest's responsibility must be complete, allowing for no rivaling interest such as comes from family ties. Schmiedeler, in his discussion of celibacy, writes:

. . . this ideal makes possible the unhindered fulfillment of the heroic works of Christian charity; and finally

---

[6] Edgar Schmiedeler, *Christian Marriage*, p. 33.

because there can be, among the unmarried, closer union with God, since their hearts are less divided and their oblation more complete.[7]

Thus Catholics may regard those who refrain from marriage in order to give themselves to a life of ministration as holding to the higher ideal of life, but the Protestant when he becomes ascetic tends to deny that any other type of life than that which he has adopted is acceptable behavior for the Christian.

So far as religion, from whatsoever motive, comes to regard sex as temptation, an appetite which should be suppressed, or a major source of evil against which war must be declared, it strikes at the basic wholesomeness of the family as an institution. Occasionally the domestic counselor comes across a marriage that has been inaugurated as a sexless relationship.[8] Such a mutilated marriage is itself evidence of a fundamental aberration which forbids an association of domestic fellowship. Tolstoy was at least logical in finally fleeing from his home because the asceticism he developed was incompatible with the normal, intimate comradeship belonging to the true family.

If, however, sex is not to be warred against, it must, on the other hand, for the welfare of Christian marriage, be given attention by the leadership of the church. It is not an impulse that can be wisely ignored any more than it can be safely suppressed. Protestantism, especially in the light of our present insight,

---

[7] Edgar Schmiedeler, *An Introductory Study of the Family*, p. 28.

[8] George W. Henry, *Sex Variants*, Volume I, p. 34.

cannot conserve the family unless it develops a more
positive factual program, a preparation for marriage
which includes sex education.

The coming of asceticism in the Christian church
does not seem so strange when we try to understand
the social situation of the early Christians, but it has
proven itself a trouble-making departure from confidence in the biblical idea of creation which expressed
a philosophy of purpose without which there could
not be a sound doctrine of marriage and the family.[9]

If this appearance of asceticism had been only an
historic episode, we might well pass it by as merely an
interesting expression of the difficulties of maintaining
balance in our thinking about sex. Unfortunately,
however, the continuing history of Christianity reveals
that not only did this outgrowth of asceticism become
a source of the discoloring doctrines of sex that have
hampered an intelligent program of church teaching
but also that it attracted many individuals possessed by
the morbid reaction which insists that sex is by its
nature base and unworthy. This false attitude toward
sex, incorporated in the Christian program, created an
unnatural and untruthful conflict. It has also prevented, or at least retarded, the giving of an adequate,
intelligent, and honest preparation for marriage. Marriage success has been achieved in spite of this, but
domestic values have been antagonized by a needless,
dualistic code of conduct.

These are illustrations of the fact that the principle
of action and reaction, of extreme right and left, oper-

----

[9] Emil Brunner, *The Divine Imperative*, p. 364.

ates in the field of sex as elsewhere. Christianity will always resist a way of life that makes sex interest a commanding motive. This will not necessarily be because of any ascetic trend, but because the overstressing of sex seems disproportionate in a life given to spirituality. This fact raises the question whether we are now living in a time when, because of reaction to a former attitude, sex is being given too much attention. The psychiatrist and the marriage counselor will find it difficult to believe that there is too much concern regarding sex adjustment. However, even these who are constantly obliged to face all sorts of problems of sexual maladjustment are likely to admit that under happier conditions sex could function as a matter of course and, as a result, many of the present conflicts, nervous afflictions and aberrations would disappear. Under the conditions of a highly complex society it is unreasonable to expect sex to function as does an uncoerced animal instinct. Nevertheless the right attitude toward sex would lessen considerably the problems of which there is a growing consciousness.

The task of the Christian church in efforts to serve family life is, therefore, neither to war against sex nor to encourage its usurping the supremacy in the man and woman relationship which rightly belongs to the love that alone offers substantial support for successful family life. The minister, as he seeks to conserve marriage and the family as a teacher and a counselor, should be concerned with sexual maladjustment as an obstacle to wholesome husband and wife fellowship.

He needs always to avoid giving the impression that sex adjustment is an end in itself or that, however successful it can be, it offers a basis for continuing satisfaction. The most serious of all incompatibility comes from the failure to carry the sexual relationship into the larger cultivation of love.

Nothing can be more important in attempting to interpret Christian asceticism than to remember that it was primarily a positive and not a negative reaction to life. This was well brought out by a question accredited to a follower of Christ who had turned his face against ordinary life. A man said to the Christian, "What is this which we read, 'straight and narrow is the way?' " He is said to have answered:

The straight and narrow way is this—that we do violence to our thoughts, and for the sake of God cut off our desires. This is what is written of the apostles, "So we have left all and followed Him." [10]

To the modern reader, ascetic sentiments are likely to seem chiefly a running away from life. This, however, was not the way the early Christian ascetics regarded their decisions. They were not concerned with ordinary things, in order that they could be more thoroughly committed to what seemed to them values supremely greater. Because we differ in our philosophy of life, we must beware of reading into their actions what their program would mean to us. We do not feel that we are in the dilemma of having to withdraw from ordinary life in order to remain spiritual.

---

[10] James O. Hannay, *The Spirit and Origin of Christian Monasticism*, p. 106.

Therefore, any ascetic trend on our side is a repudi-ation of earthly interest because of a pessimistic con-viction, rather than the sort of appraisal upon which the early Christian's program rested.

One reason for the ascetic program of the Christian church in the first centuries was the desire to cling to the apostolic period. We still find within both the Protestant and Catholic churches individuals who struggle to reproduce the situation which historically could only exist at the beginning of the Christian faith. These persons assume that the first expression of Christianity must be duplicated in every period of time. Although this cannot be accomplished because the past can never be perpetuated, a futile struggle to repeat the reactions of the first centuries of the church is possible even though it demands an artificial and self-deceiving program. Just how much of the apostolic period is timeless will always be a question about which Christian believers will differ. Nothing, however, is more clear in life than that a willful attempt to relive an adaptation to life in accord with conditions that once prevailed but no longer exist leads to needless struggle and conflict and encourages self-deception.

The critic who seeks to indict Christianity for its intermittent ascetic crusading may well consider one fact which cannot be ignored in any attempt at ap-praising the practical influence of church doctrine. Whatever was true of the ebb and flow of asceticism at any period, the thought of marriage as an ideal was secure at all times on account of its scriptural anchorage. Matrimony could be resisted or discounted as a desirable relationship for those supremely committed to the faith, but it could never fall into general disrepute. Its idealization always persisted, since from the concept of marriage had been drawn the most impressive description of the spiritual status of the church. The deeper meanings of ideas are always found in the emotional penumbra gathered about them, and nothing was more expressive of the feeling of the saints or so certain to check militant asceticism as words such as these:

And Jesus answered and spake again in parables unto them, saying, The kingdom of heaven is likened unto a certain king, which made a marriage feast for his son, and sent forth his servants to call them that were bidden to the marriage feast. . . .[11]

Let us rejoice and be exceeding glad, and let us give the glory unto him: for the marriage of the Lamb is come, and his wife hath made herself ready. And it was given unto her that she should array herself in fine linen, bright *and* pure: for the fine linen is the righteous acts of the saints. And he saith unto me, Write, Blessed are they which are bidden to the marriage supper of the Lamb. And he saith unto me, These are true words of God.[12]

And the Spirit and the bride say, Come. And he that heareth, let him say, Come. And he that is athirst let him come: he that will, let him take the water of life freely.[13]

---

[11] Matthew XX: 1–3.
[12] Revelation XIX: 7–9.
[13] Revelation XXII: 17.

CHAPTER IV

The Family and Christian Character

It is important to recognize how multiplex the alliance of the family and the church may be. When we talk about the spiritual aspect of the family, some people interpret our statement as referring exclusively to the feeling element generated in the family. This is one of the chief products of normal family relationships, but we do little justice to the word "spiritual" if we regard it as stressing merely the emotional aspects of domestic intimacy. The family proves itself a faithful ally of the church by offering a unique opportunity for the translation of ideals into action.

In the development of the child the family becomes, in early years, a microcosm where he first learns adjustment to the world outside himself. Thus the family provides a preparatory training place which makes it possible for the developing personality gradually to make a wider adjustment as he travels outside the area dominated by his parents.

In somewhat the same way the family offers the Christian an area of responsibility where he can first test the sincerity and concreteness of his principles and aspirations. The closeness of family association forbids the sort of excursions from real life that spiritual ideal-ization sometimes brings. In such cases the mere feel-ing of approval of the teaching of the church brings a sense of commitment that should never be felt unless emotional experience is translated into action. The world of everyday affairs can easily be pushed into the distance so that one can enjoy a fictitious sense of spiritual achievement, but this is not possible for any-one who comes into close quarters with life because of the demands imposed by household association. On the contrary, the home enables the individual to bring his feelings and convictions to expression. The normal family shares with Christianity an emphasis of the in-dividual not to be found elsewhere. The closeness of family relationship, its emotional meaning, forces the recognition of the individuality of its members. This is not something for which the home provides but is an inevitable part of the domestic intimacy plus the interest a parent naturally takes in each child. Chris-tianity also made the sacredness of the individual per-son a major doctrine from the first. No teaching of the church was more substantially based on the spirit of the founder. It was not that Christ frequently ex-pressed regard for the individual in words, but rather that what he did and said constantly took the unique meaning of each person for granted. He never re-garded people as a mass or directed his message to the crowd. Even when surrounded by a multitude he had the genius to make each person feel that what was being said was especially directed at him. This, of course, explains not only the loyalty that Jesus was able to win but also the uncompromising hostility. His opponents felt toward him not as if he were a false teacher misleading people generally, but as if he were making a personal attack.

Occasionally Jesus gave voice to his interest in the individual. Surely the value of each personality was never more forcefully recognized than when Jesus said:

Are not two sparrows sold for a farthing? and not one of them shall fall on the ground without your Father: but the very hairs of your head are all numbered. Fear not therefore; ye are of more value than many sparrows.[1]

Life decisions were always interpreted as expressions of the individual. His counsel was as related to the special need of the particular man or woman as, in our day, is the practice in psychiatric therapeutics. One of the most detailed illustrations we have of this is the conversation of Jesus with the woman of Samaria whom he met at the well. It shows us how he taught the person to whom he was talking to explore personal experience, breaking through emotional barriers until face to face with his inmost personal life.

Jesus saith unto her, Go, call thy husband, and come hither. The woman answered and said unto him, I have no husband. Jesus saith unto her, Thou saidst well, I have no husband: for thou hast had five husbands; and he whom thou now hast is not thy husband: this hast thou said truly. The woman saith unto him, Sir, I perceive that thou art a prophet. Our fathers worshipped in this mountain; and ye say, that in Jerusalem is the place where men

---

[1] Matthew X: 29-31.

ought to worship. . . . So the woman left her waterpot, and went away into the city, and saith to the men, Come, see a man, which told me all things that *ever* I did: can this be the Christ? [2]

Another example of Jesus' practice of turning doctrines from impersonal generalization to individual choices, revealing the motives of the person, appeared in his dealing with the young man who thought he had kept all the Commandments.

And Jesus looking upon him loved him, and said unto him, One thing thou lackest: go, sell whatsoever thou hast, and give to the poor, and thou shalt have treasure in heaven: and come, follow me. But his countenance fell at the saying, and he went away sorrowful: for he was one that had great possessions. [3]

In a most striking fashion tradition reveals this disposition of Jesus in his ministrations always to be alert and sensitive to the individual personality, in the story of the woman who sought to touch his clothing.

And a woman, which had an issue of blood twelve years, and had suffered many things of many physicians, and had spent all that she had, and was nothing bettered, but rather grew worse, having heard the things concerning Jesus, came in the crowd behind, and touched his garment. For she said, If I touch but his garments, I shall be made whole. And straightway the fountain of her blood was dried up; and she felt in her body that she was healed of her plague. And straightway Jesus, perceiving in himself that the power *proceeding* from him had gone

---

[2] John IV: 16–20, 28–29.
[3] Mark X: 21–22.

forth, turned him about in the crowd, and said, Who touched my garments? [4]

Family life, through its natural functioning as it recognizes each individual member, builds habits of thinking and feeling that create a favorable background for a major tenet of Christianity. Religious systems and social movements that tend to emphasize the group and disregard the importance of the individual find in the spirit of family life an antagonist. This results sooner or later in an attempt to minimize the importance of the family and to develop institutional services to take over functions formerly carried on by the family. Russia in frequent years has given us an example of this, but also eventually a recognition of its failure.

We are apt to forget that the incompatibility of domestic individualism in any program of group salvation works both ways. The family finds itself in a social environment that seeks to magnify the importance of the group at the expense of the individual person. It either has to enter into conflict with this philosophy of the mass, or to struggle against its own natural feelings and practices. The incompatibility remains quiescent for a time when a militant social passion dominates our life, as in war, in the early days of a revolution, or in the crusading period of some "ism," but soon there is a reaction. The normal spirit of the family begins to exert itself. Then the home becomes an enemy, and although the incompatibility

---

[4] Mark V: 25–30.

of two different philosophies of life may not be thoroughly conscious or expressed in words, there is created a basic schism which shows itself in confusion, strain, and even in conscious conflict.

One of the great assets of Christianity which justifies its ambition to conquer the world for Christ is the fact that it, more than any other faith, insists upon the uniqueness of each individual soul and thereby draws support from the family, oldest and strongest of our social institutions. The tendency of the family to realize the individual is universal, even though the form it takes and the degree to which it is expressed are influenced by differing cultural conditions. Christianity, therefore, wherever carried, finds in the family a relationship that supports a fundamental doctrine of the church.

There is another way in which the family offers service to the Christian program. There is in the idealism of the family and the church an unescapable illusive element. In the family it is so natural and so easily cared for by the mere ongoing of experience that we are accustomed to take it as a matter of course. At the birth of the child, the parent usually turns forward in his expectations and thereby assumes a double attitude toward the child. He ministers to its immediate needs. These are interpreted in large measure as they are related to accomplishments that, although in the future, largely provide motivation for the services rendered the child. This distant fulfillment—a product of parental imagination—goes forward as the child advances in age, so that there is always an idealism that keeps in the future while demanding services in the present. Although the parents' expectations never catch up, they are none the less substantial in the form they take and compelling in the actions they evoke.

A similar situation is found in Christian faith. This was the theme of Frederick Robertson's famous sermon, "The Illusiveness of Life." Christian leaders again and again have recognized the drawing power of a goal that always seems outside of complete fulfillment. It is possible for one to make Christian experience abstract so that satisfaction and a sense of success come from dwelling upon far-away ideals. Or, instead, one can narrow the meaning of the Christian life and tie oneself so firmly to the passing present that there is little realization of the frontier extension which permits enrichment of character through a faith that is the substance of things hoped for and the evidence of things not seen.

Domestic experience tends to hold in balance the two necessary elements of a wholesome attitude toward life—the obligations of the moment, which correspond to the good work expected of the Christian, and the faith that comes as the normal reaction to the picture the parent paints of the child's future career. Each experience modifies the other. Through his ministration, the parent reconstructs and purifies distant ideals. Likewise, through his hopes and expectations as he anticipates in his own thinking the child's later life, he gets the patience, the sincerity, and the inspiration he needs in order to meet the demands the child places upon him hour by hour and day by day.

Not only does the family illustrate how to keep together these two important complementary attitudes
toward life, it also tends to reconcile through the unity
of personal experience the motivations that again and
again have, in the doctrines of the church and the
practices of the followers of Jesus, become so separated and so exclusive that one, rather than both, have
been made to seem the substance of the Christian program. When we make good use of the family experience, we are prepared not only to reconcile but to
draw into vital union the two sides of Christian character.

Family association also, by its maturing influence,
helps to clarify and deepen idealism along whatever
line it proceeds. The intimacy of the household forces
upon us under normal conditions a four-sided contact.
We represent the present and the future in our own
personality, and in our adaptations we are motivated
by our recognition of that which is immediate and
that which is far away. This means that within domestic relations we are required to socialize, that is, to
bring into concrete expression, our underlying motives
of Christian endeavor. We not only learn to live with
others; we learn also to keep contact with personalities
in their process of growth and change.

Emotional maturity is not a prerequisite for successful domestic life, but rather what is needed is that the
fellowship of marriage and the family shall become a
maturing influence. A similar situation exists in Christian experience. One does not fulfill some requirement
without which he cannot enter upon Jesus' way of

life, but instead the needful thing is that there be that disposition which permits and encourages spiritual achievement. The individual stands where he is and grows Christian just as the husband and wife, impelled by love, develop comradeship. In both cases it is the *ongoing* that is important. In both instances, also, that which is promising and significant is a commitment of purpose and an ability to grow which carry the individual toward greater and greater maturity. Thus it is that both the family and Christianity are self-stimulating. He who enters either with genuine commitment is led onward by impulses that feed upon the relationship, bringing it toward a greater maturity.

Domestic association is always significant beyond its present content. A survey, although it faithfully describes the prevailing situation within the home, is deceiving unless at the same time it brings out into the open the underlying motivations. These are the source of the dynamic meaning of the family from which come the trends. Until these are discovered and made clear, any picture of an individual family, however accurate in detail, is only the shell. To get at the substance, we need to know the past in order that we may detect the way in which the intimacy is moving. Thus the family is similar to the individual's life. Its meaning has to be found in the frontier of the present moment. It may seem strange at first that the significance of a family relationship, at any moment we seek to know it, comes from the feeling each member has as to what is about to be. However, this is just what each of us finds to be true in our everyday experience, unless we remove ourselves from the ongoing of life and anchor our interests in the past. The family is not, as sometimes it seems, an organization that stands apart and is only added on to life, but rather a section of each person's life that can be marked off and described as if it were a separate portion of the total experience, an aspect intensely emotional.

The same conditions prevail within it that are always found when we search day-by-day human existence. The family fellowship looks toward the future because any kind of intimate association draws its vitality from purposes and expectations, reactions and attitudes, that, as they become conscious to the individual, are always concerned beyond the now, as the man or woman, although in the present, grasps at the future.

It is the fact that domestic values, like other life values, are rooted in expectancy that explains the difficulty we have when we seek to predict the success or failure of the individual marriage or home. What we most need to know are these most deeply placed expectations, something that in the domestic relationship may be compared with the faith of the Christian. It also is the substance of things hoped for, the evidence of things not seen. It is the very part of another's life that is hardest for the outsider to discover. If we ask the individuals concerned to give it to us in order that we may judge the promise of their marriage or home relationship, we get either a statement which magnifies disappointment or anticipation or, as is more likely to happen, an honest effort to describe the existing situation with the emotional drift left out because it is either resisted by, or unknown to, consciousness.

As a result we get data useful in disclosing the problems met by people who marry, and their successes and failures, statistically defined. We learn that they do or do not have a divorce, wish to separate or are happy together, establish feasible financial arrangements, and the like. The deeper meaning of all this, the real test of success or failure escapes detection, by any of the methods of study available, too frequently to permit us, on the basis of our findings, to speak with much confidence when we seek to predict the success or failure of the individual mating which is contemplated. The great question always is, in what direction will this fellowship move, determined, as it is, by the character tendency of the man and the woman and their reaction to each other in their highly emotional relationship.

One thing is certain. The more insight those contemplating marriage can get, the more clearly they can see the problems they have to face, the more honestly they can become acquainted with their own aims and desires, or—in the words of William A. White—the more they can extend the field of consciousness and bring into it the unconscious motivations, the greater their hope of success.[5] Their preparation cannot be static. Their security is not in discovering that they possess in good measure certain desirable qualifications.

---

[5] *Mechanisms of Character Formation*, p. 276.

These may give them an advantage but they cannot guarantee success. One does not marry virtues, but flesh and blood people who are led into marriage as into other activities by promises that are emotionally persuasive. The test, therefore, in any case is the feeling of dynamic success or failure in the effort to achieve satisfaction.

Without faith, we have little substance in our own association, and without some practical expression of our affection we never pass beyond the outskirts of the personalities with whom we have contact. Normally, our ideals are socialized because they struggle to find fulfillment in the ever-changing, ever-demanding association of family members. Our closeness, unless it brings enmity and repulsion, leads us toward coöperation with, unity with, and confidence in those whom we love. The mission of Christianity is the same on a larger scale. It also seeks to bring people of all classes, nations, and races into a fellowship which will establish coöperation, a sense of spiritual oneness, and belief in others, without which Christianity remains an unsocial luxury of the imagination or an unrooted, surface emotionalism which, however it fattens the ego, carries character away from rather than toward the teachings of Jesus.

Although the church, except in its occasional ascetic aberrations, has always taken a serious attitude toward marriage and the home, it has not as a rule emphasized the family as a pattern for Christians to imitate. The contribution of the family has been taken for granted just as is commonly true in our own time. When family interests have been given attention, it has usually been because of the appearance of some form of domestic weakness or from the desire to emphasize the obligation of Christians to practice their religion. The idea that the home is a nursery where Christian character may get its start is much less frequently realized. Such doctrines as those of infant damnation —an amazing perversion in the light of Jesus' statement: "Verily I say unto you, Except ye turn, and become as little children, ye shall in no wise enter into the kingdom of heaven" [6]—reveal how far from Jesus' understanding of the potential spiritual incentives of childhood the church has drifted at times.

The family also is tempted to take itself as a matter of course. For example, normal mothers do not drive themselves to self-sacrifice in the spirit of solemn obligation, nor do they make conscious and praiseworthy their ministrations, which become faulty the moment they are used as discipline or become a source of self-regard.

This ordinary working of family association is similar to what happens in the best type of Christian development. Men and women reach the highest fellowship with Jesus when they practice his teachings without self-concern or satisfaction. The normal mother-child attitude is a splendid illustration of the need of Christian virtues being spontaneous, an achievement that minimizes struggle even when originally it demanded effort and discipline. The Christian

---

[6] Matthew XVIII: 3.

mystic frequently has come to feel the need of lifting himself above struggle, but usually, unlike the mother with her child, he has found no way of doing this except by removing himself from the ordinary responsibilities of life. There is a better way, and it is a commonplace in wholesome family life. The task that the parent takes over may be, when looked at as an act by itself, tedious, arduous, or even distasteful. The willingness to go through with it, however, brings no feeling of struggle because it is a spontaneous expression of love. In this respect the home has a revelation for the practicing Christian.

CHAPTER V

Hampering Conditions and Traditions

No CIVILIZATION has more desperately needed to discover the way of Jesus than has ours. The mission of Christianity is now, as it was in the beginning, to help men and women find the true values that can be had only through vital spiritual insight. Its task is difficult because, in part as a consequence of indirect social and intellectual results of its own progress, it is confronted with a supremely efficient and aggressive material culture. Christianity is in conflict with a new type of paganism, expressing itself in modern form and possessing the resources of applied science. In its struggle for dominance, Christianity has an ally in the family, and one which it needs to recognize and cultivate. Both Christianity and the family, as spiritualizing influences, are menaced by a life philosophy that attempts to elevate material values to the supreme place in human achievement. It is, however, the genuine normal family in all its aspects that has spiritual kinship with Christian faith.

Christianity is not called upon to graft peculiar artificial domestic traits onto the family complex, but to take over the spontaneous home brought about by

79

the deep-seated impulses leading to marriage which in turn provides opportunity for parenthood. Christianity is betrayed into futile crusading when it distrusts the familiar domestic career and seeks to replace it with a system that is counted spiritual because it antagonizes ordinary human impulses. Instead, it is the proper business of Christianity to lead men and women to a domestic fulfillment that will not only enrich their human experience but help them find, through intimate fellowship, spiritual realization.

There are many influences in present social life that make it difficult for men and women to discover the domestic values. These social conditions we must seek to understand before we attempt to build an effective program of education for family life. Since they also are tied up with the problems that are brought to the pastor as a domestic counselor we must stop and explore the sources of the individual maladjustments of American domestic experience.

We all know from observation that the contribution of the family to spiritual development is not an automatic function of the institution. On the contrary, the influence of the family, as it affects the life of the individual member, may be the most serious spiritual handicap entering his life. It is obvious to all of us also that the American family is having troubles that come largely from our contemporary environmental situations. Doubtless a similar statement could be made concerning any period since the advent of Christianity, but the form that the domestic problem takes constantly changes. The difficulties that the present

American home encounters can be understood only by an analysis of our social conditions in the spirit of our time.

Since it is the obligation of the church to help the family contribute to the spiritualizing of life, thereby strengthening the most important ally Christianity has, it becomes important that we try to understand the source of the weaknesses of the contemporary home and the support that religious organizations can give. The heart of our social troubles, hurting not only home life but every other sphere of spiritual experience, is clearly a civilization that has been so captivated by its rapid material progress that it has lost not only its sense of spiritual values, but even any realization of its deficiency. This does not mean that life goes smoothly or that the individual is permitted to settle in comfort and enjoy the fruits of applied science. The opposite is true. A great multitude is confused, discontented, and even robbed of the physical advantages that modern civilization is capable of producing because coöperation and good will are insufficiently developed in a culture so lacking in spiritual appreciation that it fails to give people even the means of controlling their material power for their physical and social advantage.

It is only fair to say that we have been slowly moving away from hardship standards of life, most rapidly in the United States, and that the easier circumstances tend to weaken spiritual desire and to cloud the true values of life. To say this is merely to recognize that Christianity has always found its task favored by hardship. Since, however, by helping people in their struggles, thereby encouraging their increasing and effective use of their endowment, Christianity stimulates progress and becomes a substantial influence lifting the standards of life, it is useless to attempt to solve contemporary problems by advocating a return to the more meager material resources of other times.

It is apparent that until man has greater moral discipline, backward social movements are sure to occur in spite of a continuous advance of physical resources, bringing about from time to time the predicament we face just now—a lowering of the standards of living in the midst of potential plenty. However much we may welcome the greater seriousness that follows loss of comforts and luxuries, however much we may approve the awakening of spiritual appreciation that seems to come from a great social or international crisis, it is futile for Christianity to take comfort from these spasmodic occurrences of greater spiritual appreciation. The strength of human curiosity, now finding its supreme expression in science, offers no reassurance to those who believe that material progress is necessarily a spiritual menace. The only program that offers any security to Christianity is that which seeks to help men make proper use of material resources without being blinded spiritually by the satisfactions that come from an increasing control of nature.

Science itself is neither mischievous nor morally creative. It increases man's power, thus offering him new opportunity, but it is abundantly clear that human nature, to make good use of multiplying resources, must have increasing discipline and good will. The advance of science in itself cannot conserve the American family. Only the dogmatist would be sure whether on the whole our family life is worse or better than that of previous periods. There should be, however, complete agreement that American family life is blighted in a multitude of individual homes because its members are not prepared to make the best use of the resources American civilization brings them. We are not so foolish as to choose the home life of the underprivileged for our example because, although it has its deficiencies, we also know that instability, discontent, and domestic barrenness are reflected in the life of American people on every economic level. Indeed, one gets the impression that the most precarious home life of all is to be found among the wealthy. It is better, however, to give up any effort to discriminate the differences between classes and to recognize that we are all in trouble together. The impact of a dominant materialism is making it difficult for each of us to realize in our own experience the satisfaction and value of domestic relationships.

It is easy to point out much that has happened to change and to lessen the functioning of the family. These occurrences can be used as explanation of the failure of the family, but this analysis of causation easily hides what we most need to notice. The essential function of the family is found, not in activities forced upon it as an economic or vocational organization—the sphere in which the home has had the most lessening of functioning—but in the intimacy of craving for fellowship which has all the greater opportunity for realization as the family gives over the other services once essential for the maintenance of life. When conditions force upon the family this latter functioning, the activity may strengthen the home and even assure unity of effort among its members, but this by itself does not develop the deeper unity of fellowship which the achievement of spiritual values through the family demands. The genuine strength of the family is disclosed only when this external pressure is relieved.

Our present plight comes not from the giving up by the family of activities once essential to its survival but rather from the inability of individuals to surmount external competition, to handle leisure intelligently, and to pass beyond the utilization of husband and wife for physical or economic purposes to the point of finding through fellowship the satisfactions that come when members of the home are valued not as producers, superior servants, or income-bringers, but as persons who are loved for the worth they have, independent of any material contribution that they may make to the domestic group.

Family life may be made more difficult by the passing of the conventional kitchen because domestic habit is forced to make radical changes, but the cooking of food, even the serving of meals within the privacy of the home does not secure the vitality of family life any more than does the sewing of the clothes that the family members wear. If it is feared that the family may be so stripped of functions that it will have nothing left, the answer is that if people are prepared to discover and achieve the satisfactions from domestic fellowship, there will be an expansion of a basic function that will increase with the giving up of other activities. To interpret the family as an organization merely for various sorts of physical and economic services is a supreme expression of a materialistic philosophy of life that cannot even see the most essential feature of the home. Christianity surrenders all hope of developing the family as a spiritual ally if it allows the vitality of the home to be measured by whether it is maintaining or losing its one-time material functions.

It is in the meaning of family associations that Christianity has to find the basis of its alliance. It is called upon to support the preparation for family life that enables individuals, living in our own time and place, to achieve values and satisfactions that cannot be had outside the home. The family is a utility, but even more it is an answering of normal but profound cravings that have no fulfillment aside from the intimacy and the sense of belonging rarely found outside family relationships.

It may be more difficult to maintain the family as a social institution by developing the inner cohesion of affection than when we have a unity imposed by the pressure of external necessity. But it is likewise true that this more modern type is a superior family and better prepared to emphasize the spiritual aspects of domestic association. It offers greater opportunities for the educational influence of Christianity because its problems tend to be those that can be helped by the enrichment of character. The contrast, of course, is one of greater and less because the former family was by no means destitute of a union through affection, and the present home is greatly concerned with environmental conditions and is aided or injured by the social situation of the time and place in which it functions. Even so, there is no occasion for bewailing the changing of family functions where there is such an enormous opening for the spiritual ties of home life.

The deeper values of the modern home require more of its members than was true when family responsibility was so largely defined by each person's contribution to the production of economic security. This reshaping of family purpose challenges Christianity along two fronts. Religious leadership is asked to conserve family interests by helping to build a wholesome society, one that will be friendly rather than antagonistic to the character-making functions of domestic association. The second obligation of religious leadership is to provide the stimulation and the insight, the information and the guidance, that will enable individuals to make good use of the opportunities of marriage, parenthood, and domestic fellowship, that the greater values of the home life may be realized.

When we turn our attention to the problems of the first program it is obvious that the most significant social transition facing the modern family is the externalizing of interests. This means that ambition is chiefly directed outward and that the successes of the human career are largely measured by objective and material standards. Society, like the individual, needs to keep a good balance between an excessive introvertive and extravertive emphasis. Modern civilization has followed the course we often see when some person with inadequate education suddenly gains possession of great wealth. There is a marked expansion of life expressed in the multiplying of possessions, but seldom along with this enlargement is there any corresponding increase in the resources of the personality. As a consequence, the values that command the interests are largely outside the self.

The individual possesses more without becoming more, and not infrequently this makes his sudden enrichment, in the end, a misfortune. In such a case it is evident that the inability of the inner life to keep pace with the outer increase of power has led to a misuse of opportunity. It would be unfair to insist that the American people have made no progress in learning to utilize the increasing resources provided by applied science and commercial organization. There is, however, considerable evidence that many individuals and families instead of looking to machine products as a means of living a higher, richer life have become so captive to extravertive possessions that these have themselves become the objects of desire, the expected means of bringing life fulfillment.

The result of this considerable exaggeration of extravertive values shows itself in family life. The lack of appreciation of the experiences that belong to the inner life and that, therefore, are intangible in form, throws home life out of balance; and satisfactions, in so far as they can be had, are found in the functioning of the family as a utility. This, as we have already noted, is likely to be a lessening function and to furnish to the family career meager content. We are interested, however, not so much in the feebleness, through faulty purposes, of homes that seek to meet human needs, as in the significance that this holds for Christianity and the problems that it brings to the church.

Christianity, although it has had numerous illustrations of lack of balance in the practice of its doctrines when it has overstressed the introvertive or the extravertive aspects of life, has moved forward at the center, recognizing and doing justice to both of these fundamental attitudes. In maintaining the significance of the inner life it has always found an ally in a wholesome family experience. Faith, loyalty, and love are achievements commonly gained in intimate fellowships. Those who enter the Kingdom of God carry them to a higher level.

It is difficult to see how Christianity can ever make people feel the reality of its message if they have nothing in their previous home experience to prepare them for an understanding of the spiritual attainment expressed in faith, love, and loyalty. The impotence of Christianity as a routine is easily recognized, for the gospel that concentrates on work alone and leaves out faith soon ceases to be Christian. It is, therefore, the squeezing of the inner life, its paralysis, loss of vitality, that corrupts the family of its proper function as an ally of the church. Christianity for its own welfare needs to encourage a balance between inner and outer values in the motives of social life.

As an illustration of the influences that are tending to weaken the inner life and fix attention too exclusively on matters outside the self, we have the motion pictures. In this appraisal of the effect they are having, we are not seeking to determine their influence so as to pronounce them an unmixed evil or a good, but rather we are seeking to uncover what dangers need to be recognized and dealt with lest they should menace the developing character of children and youth.

We have chosen for our discussion a powerful instrument, possibly the most effective influence that operates upon young lives. In spite of this great effectiveness, there should be general agreement that there is no serious feeling of responsibility for this creative power on the part of those who produce or portray the pictures that appear on our screen. At best they represent an art, and in frankness it must be confessed that for the most part it is an art which is motivated by profit. This does not mean that there is any desire to exploit or any other purpose than to entertain people in such a way that the box office may prosper. It happens, however, that although the motion pictures do not seek to act as a major influence over changes in our civilization, their indirect results, especially upon unformed personalities, lead them to rival the church, the school, and the home. Language, dress, code of behavior, ideas, and especially standards are portrayed from the screen and become a part of the life of those who come for entertainment.

In spite of the fact that the moving pictures are in their presentation highly emotional, the trend is to externalize interests, carry the attention to the external, out-of-the-self world. The individual may identify himself with some terrific passion which is reflected by the actor, but this does not cultivate the inner life. It merely provides an outlet for a feeling that is externalized and made fiction rather than reality. This easily becomes a menace to normal development, smothering inward emotional growth.

It would be foolish to attempt to indict an enterprise with such wide and variegated appeal as the moving picture industry, but this does not mean that we should fail to recognize its inherent liabilities. Although its purpose is entertainment chiefly, and those who have charge of its production seldom desire to have it anything else, it is, nevertheless, as significant a social influence as the school or the church. Producers and actors have no training which prepares them to take the responsibility for the socializing consequences of the popular appeal which they direct. They are not insensitive, however, to public opinion, and this has led them to recognize the necessity for safeguarding the industry from criticisms directed against their exploiting baser human impulses, particularly those associated with sex.

Needful as it is for social leadership to keep constant scrutiny over the quality of the plays produced, to lessen the erotic suggestions that are so easily stressed in this form of entertainment, the importance of this censorship can be exaggerated. The more significant hazard connected with the movies is inherent. It is a liability which belongs to the form of presentation and which needs to be recognized so that other influences may be used as an antidote.

The movies are without a rival in their power to direct attention outward. Even massive emotions that can only be experienced truthfully and realistically from within are given an extravertive expression of extraordinary skill. The spectator passively sees this as an out-of-the-self portrayal. This is only the supreme illustration of a continuous extravertive bombardment by the swiftly moving scenes of the screen. Not only is there lack of genuine appreciation of the meaning of experiences that can only be known in one's own inner life, but through repetition and exaggeration the individual is emotionally hardened so that the acquiring of the more genuine insight of true sympathy becomes increasingly difficult. Meanwhile there is spread before his eyes the most fascinating picture possible of external possessions, conditions, and activities.

If in a sense we can say the mind moves with attention, it is not too much to insist that the inherent danger of the influence of the movies is that they can carry the self entirely into the environment.

Any extravertive exaggeration concerns the Christian church. Those who are attempting to advance the Kingdom of God are tempted to surrender to the massive extravertive situation and interpret Christianity as essentially an organization of activities or reform. This is indeed a portion of the Christian service, but it is also true that to enable this outward expression of the spirit which makes possible the Kingdom of God, there must likewise be inner growth which cannot proceed far if there be destitution of self-life. It is use-less to expect any radical change in the moving picture industry. The limitation of any art, or any form of entertainment, must necessarily be accepted. It is clear that the moving pictures are, on account of the way they have to operate, weighted toward an extravertive emphasis.

The moving pictures cannot rightly be counted as enemies of the home or the church, but both domestic and religious experience can be greatly hampered by a culture excessively extravertive. Therefore, the motion pictures cannot safely be permitted to have dominance as an educational influence upon youth. The Little Theatre movement shows us that there is a minority of youth who desire more than passive re-hearsal of emotions. They seek self-analysis and inner appreciation as the source of outward portrayal. This gives us a clue as to how we can wisely meet the challenge of the popularity of the moving pictures as entertainment.

It is the emptiness of a social situation where little opportunity existed for recreational self-expression, plus the fatigue due to overstimulation and competi-tion in the urban environment, that largely explains overuse of the moving pictures. They are sure to hold, at least until television provides rivalry, a foremost place in the popular forms of entertainment, and this they deserve. The monopoly that they enjoy in so many communities is, however, undesirable. Although not always recognized, excessive stimulation of extra-vertive interests and desires cannot fail to check the growth of that inner experience upon which Christianity and the family both depend for the spiritualizing of human nature.

Christianity, wherever it exists, by its inherent purpose must struggle to dominate social life or it soon weakens in its integrity because of the influence of alien conditions. One of the first evidences of its increasing success or failure is found in the characteristics of family life. At present a considerable number of American homes bear testimony to the ineffectual influence of Christianity so far as these individual families are concerned. As a consequence, certain flaws appear which in turn make it impossible for these homes to contribute as they should to the social welfare. It will help us to gain a picture of the domestic problems that challenge Christian leadership if we quickly catalogue a few of these weaknesses in our contemporary domestic life.

(1) The misuse of leisure. One of the great advances that machine industry has made possible has been a considerable increase in leisure. This has come to be taken so much as a matter of course that we are likely not to realize what an important departure it is from the habit life of the great majority of people of a former period. To say that this new opportunity has contributed little to lift the character level of the average life would surely be an exaggeration. On the other hand, it is not too much to say that there has not been anything like the advantage within the home that one reasonably could have expected from this greater leisure.

Instead of increasing fellowship and welding together the members of the family, the greater trend has been toward the individualizing of experience, thereby dissipating the common interests of association. This has not happened where there has been a conscious and conscientious program on the part of parents enabling them to develop recreational fellowship so that part of the leisure is used for the common enjoyment of the family members in some enterprise in which many or all of them share. When there was less time for recreation and much less development of commercial entertainment, this family experience was not uncommon and it was certainly a unifying influence, building understanding and a feeling of relation as parents and children enjoyed together the church social, the picnic, or the amateur theatrical. The present tendency so frequently found in the modern American home is for each member of the family to go his own way in his searching for recreation, so that the family as a whole rarely functions, and this habit represents a genuine loss in parent-child relationships.

(2) Another evidence of weakness in domestic experience is the side-stepping of parenthood. Although some of us believe that the resources of modern science should be used to prevent newly married couples from assuming the responsibilities of pregnancy and parenthood too soon, or to enable the family to space the coming of children so as to make it possible to maintain the highest standards of physical health for both mother and offspring, and to educate in child nurture and training, there is little doubt that contraceptive

knowledge is being used to escape parenthood altogether. Many of the one-child families are due to accidental failure to carry out a program of childlessness. In some cases these families are compromises, the parents being willing to assume the responsibilities for one child but refusing to assume a second time what they have come to feel is a limitation of their freedom or a task that is largely a burden. This disposition strikes even at the survival of the class that has surrendered its reproductive obligations. It is not merely that these people are unwilling to be parents. The more serious evil is their philosophy of life, which prevents them from gaining a normal domestic maturity. The natural procedure that moves husband and wife onward into the experiences of parenthood is blocked and, instead, the attempt is made to hold the fellowship as an exclusive mutual relationship of husband and wife.

There are individuals who can find possibilities of growth and emotional expansion in this man-woman association so that their character development is not retarded. This, however, is not the experience of most persons, who need to be led into a larger content of domestic interests by adding parenthood to the emotions of married life. The childless family constitutes a loss, and not one that can be charged up as of concern only to the individuals who from choice or necessity have not gone forward in their domestic career. The loss to these men and women is also society's loss. How significant this is we can somewhat imagine when we think of a society made up entirely of homes without children. Even though marital happiness reached a high level, failure to fulfill the deeper purposes of the family would lead to an emotional deficiency that would permeate and distort social attitudes in every sphere of values.

(3) There are influences that hamper wholesome home life that have an economic origin. The passing of the family's former rôle as a productive unit, which has made its financial security dependent upon the employment offered by organized industry, opens the family to attack from environmental circumstances beyond its control and against which it cannot defend itself by its own efficiency or integrity. This is a considerable explanation of the instability which appears in the modern American family. A contrary cause of the weakening of the family comes from an economic ambition stimulated by prevailing notions of success, which leads to an excessive expenditure of interests and energy in vocational pursuits and a neglect of the opportunities of marital and parent-child relationships. This failure to make good use of domestic fellowship has many causes. Whatever its explanation in the individual case, it is an unfortunate deficiency, robbing the association of a function that should provide great territory for expansion, thus deepening the emotional meaning of family contact, the prerequisite for spiritual growth in domestic association.

One of the consequences of feeble fellowship is the overemphasis on sex, the attempt to build an enduring fellowship on an interest that, unless embedded in affection, is naturally transitory because it does not lead the man-woman relationship beyond itself and usually therefore becomes self-destroying. Indeed, there is nothing clearer in domestic experience than that the physical incentives that lead to mating may impel toward a marriage that offers no security for a continuing fellowship.

There are such a multitude of environmental conditions that affect family life adversely that any selection reflects personal persuasion. We have no reliable measurement that permits us in a thoroughly objective fashion to classify these conditions in the order of their significance as assaults on family life. Anyone's choice, therefore, is nothing more than a selection of illustrations of the way that unwholesome social culture antagonizes marriage and the family.

It is not good strategy for Christianity to consider any domestic problem, for example, divorce, as an evil that can be isolated from the general social situation and dealt with as an independent menace. This policy proves ineffectual because it tends to mix up symptom with cause, blocking an expression of domestic failure rather than getting at its sources. Our divorce rate provides a spectacular and impressive measurement of family instability but, even so, Christianity cannot conserve the home unless it assumes a more positive program than merely seeking to prevent or lessen divorce or spiritually to ostracize those who have sought the courts to dissolve their unhappy marriage.

Domestic failure, whatever its cause or expression, in so far as it is influenced by unfavorable conditions, gives testimony that religion must carry Christian spirit and Christian purposes into our massive social life or little headway can be made in any effort to conserve marriage and the family. Recently, in speaking at a national gathering of prominent Protestant ministers, the program maker insisted that I take, as my topic, divorce, although it was understood that I was to speak on the responsibilities of religious leadership for more adequate preparation for marriage. It was explained that my hearers were interested in the divorce problem and that unless that was made the subject of discussion I would be likely to lose a considerable part of my audience.

The obstacles that hamper the moral and spiritual functioning of the family are not to be found merely in social conditions. There are hazards in the family career, and although these are affected by our cultural situation, they deserve special recognition and an independent interpretation. One source of trouble comes from what is commonly called emotional immaturity. The meaning of this, translated into the everyday adjustments of marriage and family associations, is that individuals are emotionally unprepared for the growth in character that successful home life demands. It is not that there has been failure to reach a definite goal which, once accomplished, would guarantee success, but that there is not readiness for, or incentive toward, that ongoing which is necessary if domestic relationship is to fulfill its purpose.

We charge with immaturity those who lack the ability to move onward because they are anchored in immediate and static satisfactions. As a consequence, they not only have trouble in making adjustments that demand a continuous development but also, because even their pleasure-seeking is repetitious, they soon find themselves facing diminishing satisfactions.

Instead of reconstructing their motives in life and frankly confessing their inability to make good use of their opportunity, they charge the relationship itself with responsibility for their discontent and in many cases seek another alliance which has again only temporary zest. Their marriage career is a serial sort of polygamous searching, ending always, if given sufficient time, in failure. Because more depends on the personal relationship within the marital partnership as other functions of marriage have lessened, there never was a time when ability to increase one's emotional maturity had such importance.

One of the most common illustrations of domestic retardation appears in the sex life of husbands and wives. It has frequently been pointed out how illusive the sex impulse is. This indictment is justified only when sex, taken by itself, is made a central feature of marriage association. On the animal level limitation of sex is normal and inevitable. This, however, is not true on the human plane, because sex has taken over an enormously expanded territory. It is this annexation which enables sex to consolidate with affection and thus spread itself through a vast area of emotional and spiritual values.

Sex becomes a source of trouble in modern American married life not only because of its restriction, due to inability to increase maturity, but also as a result of unwholesome attitudes toward it. More often than one would expect at a time when there is such frank discussion of sex and such widespread exploiting of it for commercial motives, we find in both husbands and wives a deep-seated abnormal reaction to it. This usually comes from several adverse influences working together, but usually ignorance plays an important part. No one familiar with the concrete problems presented to the marriage counselor would have any doubt of this. Unfortunate early happenings and unwholesome suggestions during the formative period of early years contribute to the morbid feeling which frequently takes some expression of fear. Doubtless during childhood and adolescence sex development will always offer favorable conditions for the taking on of morbid attitudes. It is, nevertheless, clear that more efficient education, especially within the home, would greatly lessen this type of sex problem. Those who enter marriage with an unsound feeling toward an essential element of the association are prone to have trouble in their adjustment. The larger hazard, however, is that they attempt to sever sex and affection. Feeling as they do about sex, they can hardly conceive that it is a legitimate part of the marriage relationship which by idealizing they try to remove as far as possible from an impulse that seems to them base and treacherous.

Morbid attitudes toward sex may move in the opposite direction. Then we have an exaggeration of the physical aspect of the marriage fellowship which takes on the driving power of an emotional compulsion and upon which is placed the burden of maintaining the fellowship. When sex is lifted so out of proportion, its failure to insure union is inevitable. The morbid disposition increases this certainty because it creates a division between desire and approval, and emotional conflict follows. In any analysis of a concrete problem of this sort it soon appears that we have unwholesome social influences combining with imperfect emotional development to bring about unwholesomeness. The efficient home might not always prevent adverse conditioning of sex from the outside, but even so, its teaching generally serves as an antidote, and in most cases the unwholesome social conditions would not make any serious impression on the growing life.

Immaturity antagonizes spiritual growth just as it does adjustment. The impulses that should come forth spontaneously from the fellowship of affection are aborted. This, in turn, as we have already seen, forces the relationship to build itself upon the precarious support of some ulterior motive, most frequently that of sex. This deficiency of development very clearly comes from the smothering in childhood of the religious feeling that should normally appear. It is not merely that the child is given no religious guidance. The spirit of the home, its characteristic emotional atmosphere, strangles in its earliest appearance emotional reactions which, if properly cultivated, would take on religious significance. This immaturity is, of course, not as a rule the deliberate, purposeful choice of the parent. It is rather the consequence of the spiritual emptiness of the family association. Thus the destitution of the parent is passed on and becomes a deficiency of the child. Moreover, it is well to notice that the tendency is cumulative. Whatever traditions of religious experience there may formerly have been in the family history, they lesson as each generation grows more distant from any vital spiritual experience. This void in emotional development is then filled with some other interest which attempts to act as substitute for the religious need of the members. Then the home, instead of being an ally of the church, acts as an obstruction, and the advance of the Kingdom of God is thereby made more difficult.

Part II

THE CHURCH AS AN ALLY OF THE FAMILY

CHAPTER VI

The Church and Education for Family Life

IT MAY be well for us to pause a moment and summarize the line our thinking has already taken. The family has been interpreted as inherently spiritual. It constitutes, therefore, because of its essential functions, a spiritual partner of Christianity. Its present contribution, however, is hampered by adverse influences, originating in our social environment and also as a consequence of personality defects that result in domestic maladjustments. It is obvious, therefore, that the church cannot safely look to the family to support its purposes unless at the same time it assumes the obligation to help the family function in a wholesome manner. The family has embedded in it spiritual possibilities, but these need cultivation. The family becomes for the church both obligation and opportunity. The help the church brings the family chiefly takes the form of education for family life and domestic counseling. The first of these now concerns us.

It is well for us, if possible, to come to a clear agreement as to the purpose of any educational effort to conserve marriage and the family. The program of the

Christian church is certainly not an attempt merely to perpetuate any individual family. Assuming responsibility for the giving of instruction in preparation for marriage and the family, it starts with the presumption that any home deserves strengthening. This prejudice in favor of the institution must not blind us to the necessity of breaking up a home in individual cases for the welfare of all concerned. This fact is recognized even by those who do not believe that the Christian has a right to encourage divorce. Children sometimes must be removed from the parents in order to protect them from the menaces of a bad home, and the separation of spouses may also be indicated for the good of one or both. It is important, therefore, that Christian teaching should not be maneuvered into such an expression as to carry the suggestion that the individual family, by its mere existence, establishes its value and must be maintained.

It is possible to drive so heavily against divorce as to create the impression that there should be no facing of the realities of the demoralizing family or marriage, and to imply instead that the institution commands the interest of Christian leadership rather than the quality and consequences of its functioning. Christian teaching, as it concerns the family, must avoid the suggestion of unwillingness to face family situations realistically. Nor must it be so committed to the maintaining of the institution, through hostility to the idea of divorce, as to insist that the individual exist for the institution rather than the institution for the individual. It is not enough that this extreme attitude should not be accepted as Christian principle. It is needful also that there be such clarity concerning this matter that no one will have any reason for believing that the chief purpose of the church's effort to educate for family life is to perpetuate and enforce the institution of the family with a sentimental disregard of the actualities of individual domestic experience. Otherwise the domestic teaching of the church will run counter to the moral convictions of those who know the demoralizing influences of evil family life at first hand.

Christian teaching must also avoid giving the impression that the first virtue of familial experience is fidelity. Fidelity is indeed of profound value and deserves a greater meaning than it is apt to carry to most persons. Usually it has tied into it the notion of meeting obligations, of fulfilling the law of social custom or political enactment. The reason why it should not be pushed forward as the central purpose of domestic achievement is the fact that it is itself a product rather than a cause. We desire fidelity but we want it because it is the natural outcome of an underlying love. When affection is absent, although fidelity is still desirable and praiseworthy, it is a faint attainment in comparison with a loyalty that is rooted in love.

Christianity from the first has insisted that works without faith are dead. This principle must be recognized in the domestic sphere. If teachings that strengthen the home so stress faithfulness that the idea is conveyed that the right kind of home can be established only in the spirit of duty, the deeper meaning of domestic fellowship is hidden. The task of the church, on the contrary, is to lead men and women to the realization that only through abundant and abiding love can they gather much of the values that should come from their association. The mere keeping of vows, although deserving of respect, represents a feeble accomplishment and one that does not permit the family in any great degree to function spiritually.

It is particularly important that the Christian teacher should never insist upon some standardized type of family experience. The good family is not some particular type. The family, as an organization, would offer little to human nature if it represented such a coercive organization as would come from forcing all family members to assume a conventional rôle. The power as well as the genius of the family is rooted in the fact that it offers in each individual mating a unique adjustment, building an association which can satisfy different kinds of persons, and persons on various levels of emotional maturity, intellectual endowment, and social background. It is true that an ideal family life can be safely presented, but always with this interpretation should go the suggestion that the normal form of the family permits any adaptation that individual possibilities require. It is most unfortunate to enlist well-meaning men and women in fruitless struggles or to give them any basis for the feeling of domestic guilt or inferiority as a result of their falsely assuming that as Christians they must build a standardized type of home life.

The true home is a process. It consists of intimate association in which adaptation goes forward, thus producing a common fund of habit relationship, feelings, and satisfactions through which individual traits are clearly discerned. This is true even if one insists that the different types of family life have distinct values and that one domestic expression is superior to all the others. The evaluation is social rather than particular. It is what one would like to see rather than what actually exists. Idealization is helpful, but not if it creates frustration, an unwillingness to make good use of present opportunity because ambition is directed toward something far off, the realization of which is conceived of as independent of the immediate desires and needs of the persons concerned.

This particularizing of the family must itself escape generalization. The adaptation is of husband and wife, of child and parent. It necessarily avoids the exploitation of personality which always follows an effort to impose from the outside domestic qualities that must in each person generate from within and which represent compromise and adjustment rather than conformity or dominance. The good family is characterized by zeal and resources for pushing forward rather than by the idea that the proper goal of Christian endeavor in the field of domestic relations is the achievement eventually of a stereotyped standard of home life.

The impression is sometimes given by preachers and writers of books that the Christian family has a uniformity that marks it off from all other domestic experience. There is, however, no one Christian family. In times past missionaries occasionally have been painfully forced to recognize this fact. Whenever we portray Christian families as possessing a universal similarity, it is not difficult to detect how much our description is influenced by individual experience and the social situation of our period and place. The Christian family does not surrender its necessity for individual self-expression, but its compromises and adaptations take on a distinctive relationship merely because, on account of its convictions, such a family assumes seriously the task of practicing the principles of Christianity within the household. But if this is not made clear by the teaching of the church, needless feelings of failure are experienced and guilt feelings encouraged.

It is especially important that in our teaching in preparation for Christian family life we do not assume that our task is to import into the family sentiments and motives that are alien but need to be implanted so that spiritual experience may be achieved. Our thesis has been that the family is, by its essential traits, a source of impulses that lead toward the spiritualizing of life. If this be true, the Christian program calls for a teaching which seeks to release these spiritualizing impulses and to direct them in such a way that they may find constructive realization. This conception of the purpose of the teaching program is fundamental. The opposite philosophy is sure to show itself in the technique of instruction, and most significantly in the suggestions conveyed. The modern family is a cultural product that is far distant from its primitive predecessor, in which the organization was primarily the means for taking care of the reproductive and the productive interests that made survival possible. We cannot in these days fulfill human need through functions that center about finances, sex, or childbearing. Instead there are deep-seated cravings that provide the raw material for spiritualizing experience. They are not evoked by some special marriage or family event only; they are the continuous inner drive for fulfillment through intimate fellowship. They appear forcefully in courtship, replace passion with sexual comradeship, and thus give the relationship the basis of permanency. They rise high in the consciousness of parents when a child is born and show their strength whenever the family or any of its members face a crisis.

Doubtless this interpretation of the family will seem distasteful to some who like to think of our spiritual possessions as barricaded from ordinary life. Their attitude, however, is unfortunate not only because it covers up the greater meaning of the family but because it distorts Christianity itself. This realization of the potential spiritual achievements of the family is expressed in the doctrine of the sacrament of marriage. The Protestant who finds this preachment unacceptable should at least appreciate that it is an attempt to recognize the inherent spiritual significance of marital fellowship.

The minister, simply because he has strong convictions or even a very vivid and beautiful family experience, is not thereby qualified to give instruction in preparation for marriage and family life. The family as an institution has a content of its own and any instruction to help people build the right kind of home life should at least give evidence of a serious endeavor to understand contemporary domestic experience. I believe also that the minister is obligated to know something about the science of domestic relationships. He is far too prone to pursue his reading in books that are written to cater to his assumptions and prejudices. Often you will find in his library a few books on marriage and the family, every one the product of persons who share his professional attitude. The consequence is that his teaching easily becomes exhortation and does not in any sense reflect the investigation of the scientist.

We do not expect the minister to take the objective point of view that the scientist struggles to maintain, but it is difficult to see how any instructor can be trusted who gathers his knowledge either from personal experience or from sources that reflect subjective predilection. No one asks him to teach as a scientist, but he cannot faithfully instruct if he divorces himself from scientific literature. He also needs to have familiarity with material which he is not likely to attempt to interpret but which influences his insight when he does teach. There is at the present time a considerable gathering of factual material that appears in medicine, psychology, and psychiatry, which he cannot ignore without running the risk of making his instruction unsound.

Since the minister is generally well qualified to deal with the specialized religious aspects of the family, it seems unfortunate that he should so frequently content himself by reading along these familiar lines and should abstain from the different sort of presentation that flows out of science. To be sure, he may be repelled by the fact that scientific literature gives little recognition to his special interest, but this fact makes such books all the more valuable because, instead of catering to the realm where he is already competent, they reinforce him in the territory where he is professionally weak.

It is not enough, however, for the minister to build a background by reading the scientific literature devoted to marriage and the family. In order that he may be a safe teacher, it is highly desirable that he have contact with specialists in other fields. In the small communities this may be limited to the physician. Even so, it is most important that a coöperating relationship be established. The advantage of this appears clearly in the minister's service as a domestic counselor.

Just as the pastor has reason to send his client to the doctor, so likewise, in order that his teachings may have the strengthening that comes from the experience and knowledge of the man who works in the field of medicine, the minister should seek opportunity occasionally for discussion of marriage problems as they appear in the field of medicine so that he may gain information concerning new discoveries and insight evolving from this science. Not only will this give substance, caution, and greater usefulness to the minister's teachings; it will also increase his sympathy with the work of the natural scientist. As a result, his instruction, without losing any of its inspirational value, will tend to be more factual and more practical. This contact will prove an advantage also by increasing the interest of the physician, since otherwise the minister and the doctor may in their services seem opponents or at least partisans rather than coöperating allies.

It would, of course, be misleading for the minister to set himself up as an authority in professional fields other than his own, but this is not likely to occur if an active association is maintained with someone working in another field. In the city the minister has a wider area of professional specialities from which to draw support. It will prove a good investment of time for him to maintain association with men and women in other lines of work whose approach to problems of marriage and the family are necessarily different from his own. Indeed, it may appear desirable to go still further and invite some of these specialists to share the responsibility for the giving of instruction. In such cases, however, the minister must be sure of their level-headedness, their ability to interpret to the lay person. It certainly is not enough to know that an individual is an authority in his field. He must also have some understanding of the way things seem to the lay person, and a measure of ability in making complex things simple, and above all freedom from exaggerated or morbid suggestion.

The minister's teaching takes many forms, and these need to be distinguished and interpreted. He will occasionally give instruction that is applicable to family life and marriage in his sermonizing. Sometimes he chooses to preach a sermon that is entirely concerned with domestic life. More frequently, in dealing with some other subject, attention is given to some aspect of family relationships or some insight is presented as a by-product of the discussion, that has appeal and significance for those who are married or for those who are parents. If the minister maintains interest in the family as a spiritual ally of his work, it is the most natural thing for him to include family interests in his messages to his people. He will not depend upon formal opportunities for this attention to the family, although he is almost sure at some time during a year to make the family a central theme.

The greater part of his sermonizing is likely to seek two objectives so far as the family is concerned. One is to give inspiration and incentive to those confronted with family difficulties, and especially to keep them aware of the values that should come out of home life. The second is the encouraging of an interest in the resources of science for domestic adjustment, thus creating a demand among his own people for a more specific type of instruction.

The church school can be used, and is widely being used, to deliver information and insight at various levels of experience. There are two periods of life that seem to be especially favorable for this instruction. The first is found in the adolescent group and we already have some classes that are making a serious effort to discuss problems of courtship and preparation for marriage. The other group that is most promising is made up of those who have recently married or who are about to marry. Sometimes the two sets are grouped together and sometimes they are separated. It is clear that this second group requires more factual information than those who are concerned as adolescents in a more general way with the problems of courtship and the idea of marriage.

The minister may find that he needs to have help from others, at least occasionally, in giving instruction to those who are either very close to, or actually in the midst of, various forms of marriage adjustment. Some Sunday schools have found it an advantage to use a popular text. It is my conviction that when this is done it is highly desirable that this material be presented in the spirit of science rather than that it be loaded with Christian preachments and idealization. Not that the latter can be excluded but rather that the teacher of the class must not take refuge from the concreteness of realistic situations by what so easily can become unprofitable, unsubstantial sentiment.

Another service that needs to be much more stressed than at present is the bringing to the church of lectures, by qualified persons, that have to do with various aspects of marriage and the family. It does not seem too much to prophesy that the time is not far away when this service will be greatly increased in all communities. It may not be done by the churches or it may be only partly carried on by them. The school offers opportunity. It may be, however, that there will be in every community an organization for the purpose of conserving the family.

This was the idea of Paul Sayre that led to the or-

ganization of the National Conference on Family
Relations. At present it seems too ambitious a program.
But we must remember that society, once it becomes
conscious of the tragic need of better instruction for
marriage and the family, and of the resources now
available for the giving of this instruction, may develop in many communities family councils to take
over this responsibility just as Chambers of Commerce
or Boards of Health have been organized for the purpose of dealing with commercial and sanitation interests. There is already a very considerable instructional
service carried on by such organizations as the State
Department of Public Welfare, the State Board of
Health, the Extension Division of the State University, and many other public service organizations.

It is possible that the church should offer a place
for some of these specialists to lecture. On the other
hand, it may seem in the long run important that the
church itself develop, as it has already in some degree,
its own corps of speakers. These individuals should
have something more than religious zeal, skill, public
appeal, and familiarity with the more superficial literature of marriage and the family. They need also to
be well versed in the background of the science of
domestic relations as it shows itself in medicine, law,
biology, psychology, psychiatry, and sociology. If
this substantial equipment is lacking, it is doubtful
whether, in the long run, church speakers can meet
the competition of those who are well trained in the
science of family life.

One of the largest opportunities given the minister

in his teaching rôle is offered by special classes. The one we find most common is that made up of those about to marry. This type of instruction is the one that has been most stressed by church organizations. It has become a growing conviction that the minister is obligated to give counsel to those who come to him to be married. Often this has to be personal conference, and the minister becomes more a counselor than a teacher. There is, however, especially in the larger churches, a great need of the organization of a class composed of persons who plan soon to marry or of those who have recently married.

Although it may well be said that any preparation given at this time comes at the eleventh hour, we must recognize, on the other hand, the advantage that comes from the young people's being ready for a more serious facing of their problems than could previously have been true. Doubtless when good instruction already has been provided there is less need of this special class program. At present there is considerable variation in the way these classes are conducted and also in the content of the instruction. Anyone who has had experience in this type of teaching will bear testimony that the young people are exceedingly eager to get any help they can and are unusually appreciative of the effort of the instructor.

Since at present a minority of churches are giving this service, leadership may wisely concentrate on this type of teaching. There is nevertheless very great need of special classes that represent other domestic interests. In each community and in each church the question whether there is genuine need of the following classes can be answered only in the light of the prevailing conditions. It will be found less often than one would expect that facilities already exist in the small communities for the giving of instruction along these different lines. Frequently there is little done for those who are concerned with these problems.

(1) *Marriage adjustment* in its various aspects is one of the most important of these. Men and women who face difficulties in their marriage experience welcome instruction, provided it covers so large a ground as not to disclose the particular problem of the individual and make him feel self-conscious. No matter how efficient the instruction is that anticipates marriage relationships, problems of various sorts normally appear in the progress of domestic fellowship. It proves a great advantage to have these opened up for discussion.

(2) *Pregnancy* is another interest that deserves specific attention when there is no community organization that provides instruction which centers about childbirth. The minister will probably feel incompetent himself to give instruction to a group of men and women—for it may well include men—who wish to prepare for the coming of a child, especially a first child. He can, nevertheless, be the leader of the enterprise and find a competent person to give the instruction. It seems likely, however, that this contribution to domestic welfare will for the most part proceed outside the churches. The minister by his influence can contribute heavily to the success of classes in prepara-

tion for pregnancy by stressing to his people the value of such classes.

(3) *Child training* occasionally also needs to be recognized through special classes. This is one of the oldest and therefore best developed of the various forms of specialized teaching in the field of the family and it is safe to say that as a rule the church does not need to organize this type of instruction. Nevertheless, some churches will find such teaching a very significant obligation.

(4) There is another problem that is becoming pressing, and one that has had relatively little attention. This comes from the changing character of our population, the increasing number of *aged people*. There are two parts to the problem. Those who are old need to have special help, that they may make the best possible adjustment to their increasing years. Then there is the problem of those who have in their homes fathers and mothers who have become dependent on account of their age. A great deal of misunderstanding, friction, and even tragic conflict can be avoided through greater insight into the domestic problems naturally presented by great differences in ages among members of a family. The minister is well fitted to handle classes that deal with the problem of old age.

The Young Men's Christian Association of Boston was one of the first Christian organizations to develop a program of preparation for marriage and family living. It is interesting to see the courses it offers for this current year. There is one for youth which emphasizes problems of courtship and selection of a mate; one for the recently married; and, most remarkable of all, one for fathers. The description of each of these follows. The publicity of the last is given in full because it is especially interesting and suggestive.

LIFE BEGINS IN THE TWENTIES
Leslie Updegraph and Guest Speakers

As soon as you enter your twenties you begin making decisions which largely determine the pattern of the rest of your life. Love leaves the puppy stage and you begin to think seriously about marriage. Decisions have to be made about your career—both as to getting a job and getting ahead in a job. A new social life has to be carved out, with the old gangs breaking up. In other words, life really begins in the twenties.

Mr. Updegraph, with the assistance of experts in sex, psychology, and vocational guidance, will help you to make intelligent decisions about life-planning. Frank talks about the psychological and physical aspects of marriage, personality development, social success, and vocational planning will give you a sound background for making the important decisions of the twenties.

WEDNESDAYS, 7 to 8:30 . . . Beginning October 15th

MODERN MARRIAGE
(Psychology and Sex)
Lester Dearborn

This group is designed for up-to-date young married and soon-to-be-married people (together or individually). The first four weeks will be concerned with a frank discussion of the modern point of view about sex and the physical side of marriage. In the remaining four meetings Mr. Dearborn will go into the psychological, financial, occupational, and family relationship factors of successful marriage.

The spirit of this course is the discovery of greater horizons of happiness in marriage through knowledge.

Make your marriage the fullest and richest possible.

MONDAYS, 8:30 to 10 . . . . Beginning October 20th

BEING A FATHER
A Seminar for Young Fathers and Fathers-to-be

Monday evenings, 7–8:30
October 20 to December 8, 1941

The Association School
Y. M. C. A.
316 Huntington Avenue,
Boston

With the coöperation of the Massachusetts Mothers' Health Council

WHY. . . .

In business you would not start out on a new venture without learning all you could about it in advance.

Surely you want to do as much for your child.

In the modern point of view, having a baby is a joint affair. The husband has an important part to play in pre-natal care—and the father is a king pin in child care.

Take time now to learn how father can help make mother and baby happy, healthy and wise.

WHO. . . .

The men who will be sitting around this seminar table will be vital young husbands who want to learn to be the best fathers possible. Some of them have just begun to think about starting a family; others have one well on the way; and others already have part of their family and are thinking of enlarging it.

William E. Watts, of Harvard Medical School, is the leader of the course.

WHEN. . . .

Monday evenings: 7–8:30; eight meetings starting Oct. 20. . . .

THE PROGRAM

October   20:   The Physical and Psychological Background of Having a Baby
—*Somers H. Sturgis, M.D.*
October   27:   Things for the Baby
—*Mrs. Margaret Walter, R.N.*
—*Robert E. Low*, Woodcraft Instructor
November 3:   Handling the Baby (Demonstration and practice with "Little Herby" the rubber baby)
—*Mrs. Margaret Walter, R.N.*
November 10: Keeping the Baby Well
—*Lendon Snedeker, M.D.*
  Film "From Morning Until Night"
November 17: Education Begins in the Cradle
—*Philip Solomon, M.D.*
  Film "By Experience I Learn"
November 25: Stages of Development
—Discussion led by *William E. Watts*
  Films "Now I am Two" and
  "Stages of Child Growth"
December   1:   Mother, Father, and Child
—*George E. Gardner, M.D.*
  Films "The Study of Infant Behavior" and
  "Early Social Behavior"
December   8: Open Forum
—*Somers H. Sturgis, M.D.*
  Film "The Birth of a Baby"

The Y Paterquiz

What part do you have in making maternity safe for your wife and baby?

What psychological effect does pregnancy have on your wife?

How should you select the doctor?

Should you go with your wife to see the doctor?

What symptoms should you watch for?

What kind of life should you lead during pregnancy?

What can the forgotten father do to help the over-anxious mother?

What furniture should you have in the house ahead of time?

How can you help best after the baby arrives?

What can you expect of your child at different ages?

How important is habit training and what form should it take?

Is spanking ever justified?

How can you avoid spoiling your child?

How can you best enjoy your child?

Should he suck that thumb?

These and many other questions—the ones that come up with your child—will be answered by experts in this course.

The minister, even in the large city, may not have enough interested people to draw upon to justify classes similar to these each year. Every other year may be a wiser choice, especially for the pastor of a village or rural church. The minister should usually include in any family-education program instruction for youths and for those recently married or about to be married and he should also consider whether there is need of classes for mothers and for fathers or, as often would seem more advantageous, for parents.

At the present time there is no place where coöperation between Protestant churches can be more beneficial than in the carrying on of various forms of instruction for the strengthening of family life. No particular minister can be severely criticized if he is not especially gifted for the giving of this instruction. Moreover, many classes will be too small to justify the expenditure of the time and energy necessary to make them successful if each church attempts to maintain its separate organization.

It would seem a very practical expression of the Christian spirit in many of our communities to develop a coöperative program that will distribute responsibility and particularly open the way for usefulness to ministers who have proved themselves especially skillful and helpful in delivering specialized instruction for family life. There is no inherent reason why there should be suspicion or jealousy created through the service of a minister who, by background and by interest, is splendidly qualified to take charge of classes dealing with various forms of domestic experience.

Most churches at present will find that they can help people considerably by providing them with literature that deals with marriage and the family. The books need to be chosen with the greatest discrimination and it does not seem too much to ask that each volume be rather carefully looked over by the minister. He must of course carry to his examination a broad mind and a sympathy with science. There are so many gradations of intellectual and emotional development represented in any church group that the books for a circulating library in the field of marriage and the family should represent considerable literary difference as well as various points of view.

In many churches it would be profitable once a year for the minister to act as an interpreter of the new books added to the library, for it is most desirable that the right book come into the hands of the individual reader. Some churches have taken over the task of providing literature on courtship and preparation for marriage for the young people of the entire community. Such an undertaking should be regarded as a co-operative enterprise of various churches, deserving an appropriation of money from each church. In the majority of cases, however, it is likely that the individual church will feel that it can best meet its responsibility by developing a library of its own. It is rather impressive and encouraging to find so many young people, especially when they contemplate marriage, wishing to read a book on the subject. It is one of the promising trends of our time. Often their demand can best be met not by the public library, if the community is fortunate enough to have one, but by the church library.

Pamphlets and articles as well as books should be collected for circulation. Pamphlets can be obtained from government bureaus and from social, religious and educational organizations at little or no cost. They are often concise and practical and the information is given in the form that will appeal to those who read little. Articles can be cut from magazines or secured as reprints from their authors. A good way to handle such material is to put it together according to subject and keep it in large, strong envelopes. Each collection can then be given out to those who wish information concerning its particular topic. New material can also be easily added as it appears.

It is necessary to have some system of charging the books and envelopes to those who take them out, since, if this is not done, much of the collection will soon disappear. A simple but effective way is to have each person who borrows a volume write down in a book his name, address, the title of the book or envelope taken and the date. He will then realize that there is a record of his borrowing. When the material comes back a line is drawn through this record in the book and the date added. Unless the library is very large, it is easy to see quickly what books are out at any time. The record book also shows what is popular, who has read it, and how rapidly the material has circulated. It is important to the minister to safeguard the library with the least possible expenditure of time and therefore he needs as simple a system as will prove efficient.

CHAPTER VII

The Minister as a Domestic Counselor

MORE and more church people are expecting the minister to give domestic counsel. No one familiar with the responsibilities of the pastor would be misled into thinking that this is a new departure. It is only an adaptation, in accord with the conditions of our time, of a long-existing contribution that pastors have been making. Modern young people have become conscious of the difficulties of married life and have also become convinced that persons of experience, judgment and scientific background are in a position to give help in preparation for marriage and insight for dealing with problems when they arise. It would indicate a depressing lack of confidence in the ministry if American youth were reluctant to go to their pastor for marital counsel.

Those who do ask the minister to act as a domestic counselor have three convictions that explain their eagerness to look to the clergy for help. They believe the minister is in a position to understand human problems, especially those that originate in marriage or the family. They take it for granted that his training, as well as his contacts with people in trouble, has given him a penetration that make him especially qualified to act as counselor. They also assume that he is familiar with the resources that are needed to deal successfully with domestic difficulties. Most young people think of these as coming from the principles of morality and the facts of science. These men and women come to the minister believing that he appreciates ethical values and is acquainted with whatever resources of science there may be for the working out of their problems. They also take it for granted that the minister has a keen sense of professional responsibility. They classify him with the physician in his ability to respect confidences. Frequently they expect him to be more human and more sympathetic than the doctor but an equally safe person with whom they can wisely uncover the most confidential of personal troubles.

Domestic counselors have different professional backgrounds. Each of these carries its inherent bias which easily becomes a danger in counseling service. The minister is no different from the doctor, the social worker, the psychologist, psychiatrist, or sociologist. It is important that each type of specialist recognize his professional tendency and do his best to keep his judgment and his practices from the coercion which so naturally arises from his interests. It is not difficult to find the source of the professional dangers that confront the minister when he seeks to give help to those in domestic trouble. By training and by disposition he is a person of strong moral convictions. He finds the chief values of life on the ethical level and this means that in his contact with people in trouble he has two temptations.

One is that he may regard every difficulty as chiefly moral and make no effort to analyze the influences that are acting to cause trouble. His second danger is that he may content himself with proclaiming ethical principles and do little to help the individual understand his predicament. The fact that every situation has moral meaning does not justify the minister's unwillingness or inability to regard a marriage problem as a complexity in which many influences are finding expression. A more thoroughgoing handling of the problem is needed, not merely because otherwise a true picture of the situation cannot be secured, but also on account of the value to the minister himself of this effort to dig to the bottom. Unless he becomes skilled in analysis and is willing to see a problem in other aspects than the moral, his professional inclinations will strengthen his tendency to develop the habit of seeing everything exclusively as moral.

The best way to help the person in trouble is to search for the concrete explanations of the difficulty and to discover a specific solution. Occasionally moral issues are covered up and the greatest service the minister can render is to bring them into the light. More often, however, the individual who comes to the minister for help is already convinced of the moral meaning of his situation, and this is his reason for his choice of counselor. If he is to be led out of his difficulty, he must gather, through his consultation, some clue as to the causes that have brought about his problem and also some feasible, detailed procedure that will enable him to start toward a solution. If the minister uses his counseling to get a closer grip on human nature, to have familiar contact with the ideas and the motives and the expectations that explain the behavior of people, he gathers enormous resources for effective preaching. The minister who wrestles with human nature at close quarters is able to recognize its ever-present complexities and individualities and thus to acquire an attitude toward life which is certain to come out in his preaching and to make it more appealing and helpful.

It might seem needless to say that the minister, when he assumes the rôle of counselor, must beware of becoming a judge or an advocate. Undoubtedly the act of judging cannot be kept out of the experience. The ministerial characteristics make it inevitable that a decision be made in his own thought process as to the meaning of the situation presented and the fixing of the responsibility for its occurrence. This inward judgment, however, can be kept from expression. It deserves to be part of the minister's thinking but should not as a rule become vocal. People do not come for counsel in order to have judgment pronounced.

People who give help to others always are open to the temptation to find through their service a means of enhancing their own feeling of authority. Again the minister is like others in having his special type of temptation. It is easy, but heartless, to create in the mind of a suffering, bewildered person the impression merely that he has done wrong or that he is the victim of some other person's evil-doing. The total situation may demand such moral evaluation, but it should never be true that the individual leaving the minister's presence is overwhelmed with a sense of guilt or of martyrdom rather than with the conviction that something can be done to make a bad situation better. It seems fair to say that people would come oftener to the minister for help, were they not afraid that his chief attention would be on this placing of blame.

The doctor, who may not wish to deal with marital difficulties and may not be equipped for such services, is frequently chosen chiefly because the individual feels that his pastor would be mainly interested in fixing the moral responsibility or, what is even more unfortunate, too likely to content himself with moral preachments. It is not necessary that the minister lessen his own feeling as to the significance of the moral character of the individuals included in the problem, but merely that he restrain himself from overstressing this tendency due to his realization of the importance of the moral aspects of any incompatibility or of any unwholesome social situation.

About one thing there are likely to be differences of opinion. Shall the minister follow up any case, seeking once in a while to discover what has happened, or shall he never refer to the matter again unless the person who came for counsel invites his interest again? Perhaps the answer is for the minister to find out what the client wishes at the time of the first consultation. It may be preferable to bury the matter or, on the other hand, it may be most desirable that the minister from time to time attempt to find what progress has been made until a successful solution has been reached.

The proper program should evolve from the total situation. The important thing is that the individual be helped, not hurt. He may need to feel that the subject of discussion has been closed and forever put aside. On the other hand, he may profit from his knowledge that there is a continuing interest and this may give him strength and inspiration. Sometimes, also, the individual has lack of courage to make a second visit even though this is most desirable. His first coming may have been a sudden impulse in a mood that does not again return. These differences between people and between the circumstances associated with their difficulty must be recognized by the counselor because the people with whom he deals usually have an intellectual background, a sense of personal responsibility, a self-pride that distinguishes them from a less sensitive, less self-possessed type of personality.

Unless the minister conscientiously feels that he should not attempt any counseling on account of some personal handicap or adverse social situation, it would seem that he has a professional responsibility for carrying on such service. Not only is there a great need of domestic counseling and an increasing demand for it, especially on the part of young people, but his failure to make counseling a part of his ministry encourages irresponsible persons to exploit those who seek help in meeting domestic problems.

As is to be expected, pseudo-scientists, clever but incompetent persons, are conscious of the financial opportunity which the growing demand for counseling brings. In various ways they try to build a reputation as domestic counselors. We even have on the radio people who give snap judgments to husbands and wives who are entangled in situations that require careful, thorough and lengthy investigations and analyses. Instead of this needed factual study of a domestic tragedy, judgment is pronounced quickly with no greater knowledge of the circumstances involved than the hesitant, emotional, highly subjective statements made by the nervous, embarrassed client. The chief interest of the person who is so recklessly giving advice is to appear convincing and to be as dramatic as possible. When one remembers that many thousands of men and women may be listening in, some of them confronted with what seems to be a similar problem, one gets some idea of what a menace this attempted treatment of domestic difficulties may be.

We also have an even greater number of individuals who with little background and no sense of professional ethics set themselves up as private counselors. Some of them may be shrewd and frequently helpful in the advice given, but they do not have either the serious purpose or the scientific and ethical background that justify counseling. Undoubtedly, some of them turn to blackmail as a means of increasing their income.

The legitimate domestic counselors are making every effort possible to protect people from the exploitation of the charlatan and the pseudo-scientist. The demand for counseling is, however, rapidly growing and there must be greater opportunity for help than is at present available or people with family and marriage troubles are almost certain to turn to these so-called counselors who are doing their utmost to advertise the services they claim to offer. If it were generally known that ministers perform the same service, but more competently and more conscientiously, the profits of the exploiters would soon dribble away.

In many communities the only counseling that can be provided must come from the minister. It is true that many doctors do give advice to people who are struggling with some domestic problem. Doctors are not, however, trained in medical schools for such service. Aside from what is included in their few required courses in psychiatry, doctors usually have little opportunity to get insight that will help them later in giving advice to men and women in marriage and family difficulties. Even in the field of sexual adjustment, a doctor does not, as a rule, have any instruction in the medical school that prepares him to deal with marital difficulties. He is not in his practice usually interested in domestic problems but merely gives advice because his patient asks for it, and he cannot easily avoid the demand made of him. He would much prefer to send the patient to someone else, and in many communities his only choice would be the minister.

There is, frequently, in connection with counseling, the need of medical examination or of some medical treatment. This, however, is a different sort of service from domestic counseling, and is, of course, the sort of service the physician is prepared to give. The alliance of a minister and a physician is often necessary if the client is to get all the help he needs as he struggles with some marriage or family difficulty. This desirable division of labor is, however, not possible in the community where the minister does not act as a domestic counselor.

It is neither necessary nor desirable for the minister to advertise his willingness to give domestic counsel. If he has prepared himself to act the part of a counselor, opportunities for this special type of counseling will come in the natural course of his pastoral work, and his success will encourage other people to bring their problems to him. The best possible way for him to establish himself as a counselor is to prove his worth and gain that person-to-person recommendation that competent counselors always find the chief source of the increase of clients. The minister may indeed prefer never to use the term "domestic counselor" and may not make his parishioners feel that his consultations are a special form of his pastoral work, but he, at least, should understand the meaning of what he is doing and the responsibility that it brings.

Although domestic counseling must be only a part of his ministerial program, it is nevertheless a special type of service and one that requires specific study. He is engaged in something distinct from his other work as a pastor, something that demands a special relationship and carries with it responsibilities different from those involved in any other activities. Effective domestic counseling is not to be expected unless there be recognition that this type of pastoral service constitutes a special type of professional obligation, one that must be carried through in the spirit of a specialist who is keenly aware of the ethics involved in his undertaking. The minister cannot counsel wisely unless he firmly limits himself to the territory in which he is prepared to serve. Questions of law, medicine, psychology or psychiatry, concerning which he can have only a layman's opinion, he must insist upon his client taking to other specialists. His experience will soon make him aware of the problems that rightly belong to him. He will have no desire to be regarded as an authority in other specialties although his reading and study will keep him aware of the contributions that other professional people are prepared to make to men and women struggling with domestic difficulties.

The marriage counselor, like the physician, is too often left ignorant of the outcome of the client's case. In the small community where everyone is well known, this will not be true except of strangers who come from a distance for consultation. The minister who has become well known for his counseling will have such people from outside his pastorate. In these cases he will find, as does the counselor in a sizable city, that often he will not be able to learn what finally happened, even though the husband or wife or both have promised to write him. This failure to get a final report hampers counseling because experience is the best teacher and, therefore, the counselor needs to know, if possible, the result of the service he has tried to give. In many instances, because successful adjustment follows, the person who sought help appears eager to drop even the memory of the trouble and is, therefore, disinclined to write the counselor even if he has promised that he would. This reluctance undoubtedly discloses that there has not been the complete clearing up of emotion that is desirable. However, the counselor sometimes accidentally learns what has happened in some of the cases where the promised report has not been made, and he often finds that everything suggests that there has been a satisfactory solution of the problem.

The minister who functions as a counselor in a large city will have still greater difficulty in following his cases to the end. This is true not merely because of the way the urban population moves, but also in a greater measure on account of the tendency among city people to take advantage of the anonymity which their environment encourages. The counselor, recognizing that the majority of those who come to him fail to let him know what finally happens, will never grow weary in impressing upon each client his obligation to inform the counselor as to the conclusion of the problem.

The minister who attempts domestic counseling cannot safely regard it casually as a mere by-product of his pastoral service. Whatever may be his habit regarding records of his other activities as a pastor, he must carefully make some written record of every consultation he holds. In the small community this need not be more than the name, the problem presented and a very brief summary of what the client said and what counsel was given by the minister. It should, of course, be dated. In the city there will be need of more detail in order that the counselor may later be able to recall the case and also that he may have in permanent form the information needed to interpret at a later time the character of the client and the nature of his problem.

These records are best preserved by some sort of card index system. The counselor will soon find, after he experiments a little, what serves him best. It will be desirable either to have these records in a place where no other person is likely to have access to them or, if it seems to be still safer, to number them in such a way that without the key, which is always in the possession of the counselor, no curious person can identify any case. It is highly important that the counselor always include what he says to the conferee, since this may be misstated or even misinterpreted with the possibility of an attack being made on the minister or of his becoming involved in some legal controversy. It is well for the client to know that these records are kept and that the counsel given is briefly stated in writing since this will make him more careful when he reports to someone else the result of the conference.

Some counselors tend to make a rather complete statement while others are satisfied with a very brief summary. The important thing is that a record always be made and placed on file as soon as possible after the conference has been held. Some counselors will only make a part of this record on the card during the conference, while others will practically complete it at that time. Since some clients are embarrassed if they see that what they are saying is being written down, it is the preference of some counselors to have the client write his name and address and date on the card with the understanding that a summary of the conference will be added later. The records, once made, must be guarded as conscientiously as are those of the physician.

The minister will occasionally discover that his counseling has brought him a very difficult problem of personal ethics. What his procedure is then must depend upon his conscience, judgment and realization of his obligations to keep confidential the information given him. Problems will be presented that concern several people whose interests are in conflict. If the minister cannot maintain in a particular case the confidence expected of him, he should frankly say so to the client except in such peculiar situations as those, for example, in which he is dealing with somebody who is not socially or mentally responsible.

The minister will not only need insight in dealing with the individual problems at the time of conference, but also ingenuity in manipulating people or circumstances if this seems necessary to save someone from a tragic situation. He is not so well trained to meet these problems as is the Catholic priest who is prepared, during his period of study for his profession, to deal with all sorts of baffling ethical questions brought him by the confession. The Protestant therefore must train himself to make the ethical decisions forced upon him as a result of information given in confidence. Sometimes he may himself seek counsel from others in order that he may at least get another's judgment, just as does the physician who calls in another doctor for consultation. The counselor must be prepared for anxious moments when he is forced to decide his own action in a complicated and even tragic situation. His perplexities and sympathies during such ordeals will help keep him human in his contacts and prevent his profession from ever becoming a barrier in his association with people who need help.

CHAPTER VIII

The Rôles of the Domestic Counselor

THE kinds of problems that come to the domestic counselor are beyond imagination. After a time he is apt to think that he has had thrown at him every type of problem possible and it seems that nothing new remains. He does not, however, hold to such thinking long, for suddenly he finds himself confronted with a combination of circumstances quite unlike anything else that has had his attention. Again and again he listens to the rehearsals of life experiences which, if reduced to literary form, would seem so improbable that no novelist would dare reproduce them in fiction. Even problems that are similar in an underlying difficulty have such individual variations that each has to be treated as something original and peculiar.

If one is interested in human nature and likes to explore it, no greater opportunity can be found in any profession than in domestic counseling. Not only is there a stupendous diversity in the form that human action and reaction take, but for the most part the revelation of this is given on a profounder level of contact than ordinarily appears. The counselor is permitted to go down deeply into the tragedies and the heroisms of life, and through his contact he is educated into a sympathy and understanding unexcelled in any other professional relationship.

Many of the problems that the client brings seem needless, even though they have become great because of the meaning they have gathered. One quickly grasps the fact that there was no essential reason for their development other than the mistakes of judgment, the wrong attitude, or the immaturity of one or more of the persons concerned. It seems a great pity that there should be so much unnecessary suffering. Frequently it will even appear that the problem is essentially fictitious. It is a creation of too great sensitiveness, jealousy, suspicion, or even undisciplined imagination. The counselor may quickly recognize the needlessness of the problem. The superficial foundation of this will, of course, not lead him to regard it lightly or lessen in any degree the serious thought he will give to its solution. Here, as always, the question is not, how great and real is this problem, but rather what does it mean to the persons involved and how much trouble is it making.

Some of the problems that come to the counselor fall into another category. They are recognized early in the conference as fundamental, similar in meaning to the Greek tragedies. They suggest human nature being moved about like puppets by strings that are in the hands of fate. The individuals appear overwhelmed by terrific forces which come forth from primitive emotions or from a tremendous set of circumstances, and if a solution gradually appears, it is nevertheless frequently true that someone must suffer.

It may not at all be the person the counselor would choose. Since the minister has undertaken the obligation of helping people, it is well for him thus to go down into the very depths of the character and struggles of men and women. It will take from him any tendency in his preachment to treat human motives and sentiments lightly. It will give him a patience and a tolerance that can rarely be secured in any way other than through familiarity with the sufferings and conflicts that appear in human life. It will mean not merely that he will think differently about people but—and this is much more important—he will feel more intensely and at the same time with a more profound compassion. Thus sympathy comes only through direct contact with human striving.

It is helpful to consider the ways that the counselor may function. This does not mean, of course, that at any particular time the counselor is attempting to respond to any single demand made upon him. The purpose of such a description can only be to illustrate the kinds of service for which people ask and the various rôles that the counselor is asked to fill. It may well be that he excels in one of these or has a marked deficiency in another. As a rule, however, he is likely, in any conference, to carry on along many of the lines that we can distinguish and describe.

One of the most common of these rôles is that the counselor is chiefly asked to become a listener. The individual has great need of talking to someone in whom he has confidence. He will feel better merely because he has been able, without the feeling of disloyalty or danger, to say the things necessary to release the feeling that his situation has evoked. Not only may he have relief, but in the mere process of communicating his emotion and his thinking he may find for himself the way of escape. In any case one of the most common motives that bring people to the counselor is this desire to speak frankly and with considerable fullness the words that will empty his life of a devastating emotion.

The therapeutic value of purposeful confession has long been recognized. It cannot, however, profit much if it is forced, or made a chronic morbid self-expression through repetition. It should be spontaneous and in most instances made but once. It is always difficult to be alone, and never is this such an ordeal to persons of normal sensitivity as when one is barricaded from others because of a self-imposed sentence and the necessity of keeping to one's self an emotional burden that can never be lightened unless it is shared by another.

It would be a mistake to regard this eagerness to make a confession as a sign of weakness in personality. Those who are closely associated with criminals know that there is no relation between the strength or weakness of the character and the desire to make a confession. It is the sensitiveness of the individual that chiefly decrees whether or not he is moved toward a confession. There are men and women who seem to murder with little or no emotional reaction, and who apparently have not the slightest inclination to uncover their crime, because it is no emotional burden to them. Confession, for them, has no purpose. In contrast with them are those people who are tremendously oppressed by some minor act on their part for which they feel guilt, and because of the intensity of their reaction, they have need of the relief that confession brings.

It is not, however, merely a matter of sensitiveness. In addition, there has to be some previously accepted code of behavior which makes them feel that they have violated standards that they approve. Here, again, the strength of the feeling does not by itself demonstrate that they are judging their behavior rightly and that, therefore, their guilty feeling has substantial basis. It will do them no service, especially at the beginning of counseling, to attempt to remove all misconceptions or to challenge the standards that have become the basis of their moral judgment. However wrong they may be in the way they see their situation, the pressure they have for confession demands, for their welfare, adequate expression. The counselor will not necessarily accept the implications of the confession that may exist in the mind of the troubled person. He will, nevertheless, accept his rôle as father confessor at least temporarily and make use of the rehearsal in his effort to understand the personality of the client. He will find that the confessing may have a therapeutic function even though a calmer, sounder judgment may show the conferee that there was no occasion for confession.

Surely no domestic counselor, even though he has not had much experience, will assume that a confession must always be obtained. He is in a position, if he so wills, to use his prestige and suggestion to entice the client into confessing, even though that was not the motive of his coming for the conference. It would be a mischievous obtuseness to the differences between people and between circumstances, always to require as a first part of the conference the confessing of the client. This would mean asking something that honestly could not be given. Indeed, such a procedure would be so contrary to normal conversation that it would probably put an end almost immediately to any genuine relationship between the counselor and the conferee.

It does not follow, however, that because the client has not come with the intention of making a confession, nothing should be done to get him to free his mind. If, as he talks, it becomes apparent that he has something that he is concealing, something that has become a burden to him emotionally, he should be encouraged to give free flow to his underlying feelings. Even though a confession is desirable and the counselor attempts to do what he can to bring it about, this does not mean that he will always succeed or that he should go so far in most cases as to put pressure on the person. If the client goes away feeling that he has been tricked into making a confession against his will, his reaction is likely to predominate so as to ruin the conference.

Ministers as a class doubtless tend to overidealize people toward whom they have sympathy. In the commercial field there is a common belief that ministers, like teachers, are more gullible than most people. If this is true, it is probably due largely to the limited experience in business that most clergymen possess. It is also a consequence of the fact that the minister assumes people to be honest until they are proven insincere.

In counseling it would surely be as unfortunate to have a chronic attitude of suspicion as to have the habit of overestimating human character. In many cases the fact that the minister has such strong confidence becomes in itself an incentive to the individual who had lost courage because he felt that nobody believed in him, until indeed he did not believe in himself. Nevertheless, the minister must always be on his guard lest he allow his kindly feeling to prevent the factual judgment necessary if he is to function helpfully as a counselor. He must not interpret the outcoming of emotion which merely gives evidence of sensitivity, a responsiveness which may even be neurotic, as a demonstration of the client's sincerity or determination to reconstruct his life. It may mean this but, on the other hand, it may have no lasting significance as a resolution to reshape the pattern of his life. Sometimes the individual, through a lack of knowledge or a misconception of facts, is suffering from an emotional exaggeration but, even so, confession may be his only means of escape.

The meaning of what is confessed is not to be found in the facts, as they become known to the counselor, but in the reaction that the client has made to them. So far as the individual's feeling is concerned, the real facts are subjective and they must be recognized as long as they exist in the mind of the conferee. The act of confessing may remove some of this inward interpretation, establish, perhaps, genuine objectivity. Until this happens, the way a client sees the situation must be accepted as the basic problem. The minister can recognize this without at the same time allowing himself to be coerced by the misjudgment of his client. No one in the counseling profession should be more fitted by training and ethical standards to act the part of a father confessor than the minister.

The question sometimes arises, whether the minister should check a confession that may lead later to a feeling of shame or embarrassment. It is thought by some that the skilled counselor will know when to stop the outpouring if it is likely to make the client later regret that he has been so frank. Two things, however, need to be remembered. Many of these individuals will, in any case, react with misgivings, at least temporarily, and yet they need to make a thoroughgoing confession and may never again have courage to open up the matter if they do not succeed in fully discharging their emotions. No one can be so intuitive as to know at what point the confession must be stopped lest it become later a cause of embarrassment. The minister, acting as a marriage counselor, is not assuming the rôle of a psychoanalyst who can usually function over a long period of time and who takes for granted that there will appear distinct stages representing inconsistent attitudes on the part of the patient during the period of consultations.

The domestic counselor learns to be prepared for reaction to the confessing. The client may be both relieved that he has emptied himself and at the same time sorry that he has given anybody such a frank, faithful revelation of his inmost life. The reaction does not mean that the confessing was a mistake. It does not necessarily signify that there is any feeling against the counselor.

On the other hand, at times there is a degree of hostility, or at least of aloofness. It may be true that this demonstrates that the problem has not entirely been cleared up and that the individual has not gained the mastery that full maturity permits. The confession can prove a great advantage to the conferee even though it is apparent that he is still entangled in emotions and therefore does not take a thoroughly objective attitude. To assume that gratitude always results when the individual recognizes that he has been helped is to have a naïve idea of human nature. Great and lasting appreciation may be the outcome but, on the other hand, a different type of personality may seem to be unappreciative or even to feel in some degree a peculiar resentment. It may be in the latter case that a greater maturity can be had only through a long-continued psychoanalytic treatment.

The minister may regret the reaction that the confession brought but he should not be astonished by it or blame himself. After all, his purpose was not to strengthen friendship, even though he might wish that to happen, but to clear up a difficulty. If his endeavor has lessened his popularity he should accept this reaction objectively, much as he might wish it otherwise.

The minister also, as a counselor, is asked to become an interpreter. When this is true, he is expected to give that objective point of view which the individual is wise enough to know he cannot get for himself. It helps him immeasurably to see how another person, not tied up by his own interest in the case, sees the situation. The minister may be asked to give more than a mere trustworthy judgment. Insight may be sought, which, it is recognized, cannot come except from a student of human problems who has a considerable background of experience. The individual who asks for interpretation is likely to be intelligent and ready to deal sensibly with his problem, once he understands just what it is.

One of the most effective ways of clarifying the situation is to use previous cases for illustration. The majority of people who come for help seem to be exceedingly concrete in their thinking. It means a great deal more to them to see how somebody else in similar circumstances discovered and handled a problem than to be told the same facts in a more general way. This use of the experiences of other persons has also the advantage that it does not carry any risk of being interpreted as an attack. The client is willing to have his own problem analyzed critically if it is done through somebody else's case history. It seems to take the edge off what otherwise would be resisted by some in the spirit of self-protection.

It is not difficult for the counselor, after he has had two or three years of experience, to find material for illustration. Even though no two cases are alike in all details, there is frequently enough of common meaning to make possible this use of interpretive experiences. The examples will not always come from previous counseling, because they may have become known through reading the literature. In some cases the counselor must be careful to guard against the conferee's missing the point and taking another's situation as identical with his own. This can be avoided if the counselor takes great care to point out the essential likeness of the two careers.

The minister should also function as a giver of information. The person coming for help realizes that he does not have the knowledge necessary to deal successfully with his problem, and, all too often, does not know how to get what he feels he must have, to act rationally. He therefore turns to the minister whom he trusts, believing that he is well read and either already knows or can easily get the facts that should be had. The questions asked range from matters of legal import to principles of psychiatry. The minister will often feel confident that he can give the needful information but when he does not, he should know where to get it and agree to make the effort or he should tell the client how to go to the proper authority for it himself.

The counselor will gradually accumulate a considerable file of addresses of persons who can be depended upon to take over certain types of problems. Many of these will become known to him by correspondence. He will frequently be asked. for example, where a couple marrying at some distant place can find a competent physician for a premarriage examination. Persons who have sought his help through correspondence will, by reporting the results of their interviews, add to the names of those who have been found useful and, therefore, to whom he can wisely send others for particular kinds of services. It will be necessary, however, frequently to seek through some agency names of specialists who can be recommended to a client who wishes information, examination, or treatment. Every effort should be made to check up on such visitations, especially if the recommendation comes through some distant agency. I have known cases in which the doctor suggested had retired from practice or was dead, and many more instances in which the client was dissatisfied with the service rendered.

The minister in his counseling will also find that he is being used as a source of courage. It is by no means true that a difficulty can always be resolved. There may be insuperable barriers to the course that would be pursued were it not for the fact that it involves sacrificing others. This is not an uncommon situation in a family incompatibility when the welfare of young children is at stake. It is a terrific test of character to face an irritating or revolting experience continuously, day by day, even though behind the endurance is a profound motive of unselfishness.

It is not strange that persons who have to meet a trial of this sort need to have the help that comes from the sympathy and understanding of some other person.

The minister may well wish at times that he were not chosen to become an emotional or moral support. It is hard to see, however, on what grounds he can refuse to meet such a genuine need when some person in trouble comes to him for help. He may wisely eliminate himself as quickly as this becomes possible, but if he is committed to a realistic attitude toward human behavior he will not be surprised that he is chosen as a counselor chiefly because through him a renewal of courage becomes possible.

Sometimes this inclination for emotional fortification is carried still further and the minister is called upon to become a silent partner in a terrific trial. The opportunity to get counsel is accepted for the purpose of enlisting the sympathy of the minister in such a way that he will become an ally of the one who feels that he cannot by himself carry on. This is a highly dangerous type of service. Although this is a hazardous relationship for the individual who feels overloaded with trouble, even so it may be temporarily therapeutic and a service that the minister can hardly decline to give without greatly lessening his client's hope of escape from his affliction. The minister who accepts such a situation eagerly, or who in any way, either unconsciously or with forethought seeks to perpetuate it, is not qualified to act as a domestic counselor. When he is made aware of his weakness, he should cease such service until he himself becomes a sounder sort of personality.

The counselor should be equal to the responsibility of becoming temporarily a prop for the support of another person's courage. The situation, however, needs to be clearly recognized from the start, and deliberately and increasingly the counselor should begin to prepare for its elimination. His relationship should not remain a means of establishing parasitism but instead it should stimulate self-confidence and a willingness to accept responsibility. The counselor's success should not be measured by the strength of the ties that develop between him and the client, but by his ability finally to bring the latter to the point where he can stand on his own feet. If this cannot be accomplished, whatever other good results may come, the counselor is left with the realization that, in dealing with this particular case, he has not been able to achieve success.

The technique of the counselor in his attempt to release the conferee from too great dependency will be that of leading him gradually to feel that he is taking over the solution of the problem. He must be given concrete things to do and decisions to make; and his attention needs to be directed to anything he accomplishes. He must be led to feel that his contribution is worth while and that it is something more than merely carrying out the suggestions the counselor gives. In other words, the counselor will magnify what the other does, and as far as possible, by suggestion, keep the conferee from concentrating upon what is done for him or dwelling upon the importance of the assurances he is getting from the counselor. A campaign of self-elimination becomes the obligation of the counselor, but he must not expect to fulfill his purpose by a miraculous change in relationship. This may come about, but one cannot count on its happening. Once the client frees himself from dependency, care must be taken that he is not oppressed with the fact that for a time he had to draw his emotional courage from another person's strength.

The minister may also find that his counseling is leading him to assist another in making a decision. The counselor always must beware of assuming the prerogatives that belong to another individual, for it is not his business to discover what ought to be done and then insist that it be carried through. Instead he rightly acts sometimes as a sort of psychic midwife who helps the person in trouble deliver his needed decision. The problem is that of leading someone else to the understanding and to the sense of responsibility which is required before he can decide what to do for the welfare of others as well as himself. There can be no stereotyped system of the methods for accomplishing this. The counselor's task is to open up the situation so that it be clearly realized and then to encourage the moral feeling of obligation to carry out the decision that has finally been made. Sometimes considerable time has to be expended merely because there must be a gradual building up of the reasoning of the client or the pluck that is necessary for successful handling of his trouble.

The minister may also find himself called upon to do a very delicate and difficult task. He may be invited to act as a conciliator of persons in trouble. It is at least a reasonable request to ask the minister to consider the problems of the two individuals concerned, in order that he may seek to find a compromise or an adjustment that will be fair to both of them. He will not wisely, however, promise always to carry out such a responsibility. Once he has become familiar with the situation, he may see that there is no hope of accomplishing what has been asked of him, at least for the present, and that any attempt to force an adjustment would only make matters worse, or he may finally feel that the responsibility of rendering the decision belongs to someone with a background and experience different from his.

When the latter is true, he may be able to do a great service by showing the husband and wife or the parent and child why he cannot do for them what they ask, and where they can get the insight they need. It is important that he should not give them the impression that he is trying to evade something that belongs to him but rather that he *knows* that he should not undertake what they desire. If he can make it clear why he refuses and why some other individual is better qualified, he contributes to the success of the second counselor, for he has helped the husband and wife to understand the significance of their problem.

Sometimes it behooves the counselor to make what is known in baseball as a sacrifice hit. He takes over the case and seemingly fails. The client finally reaches the solution and discounts the value of the part the counselor played. Someone else is given credit for bringing about a satisfactory adjustment. It may be, however, that the counselor's part was indispensable. It was nec-

essary at the beginning for someone to carry through
what was of importance merely because it paved the
way for someone else later to do the necessary service.
This may mean that a certain mood had to be dislodged
or uncomfortable feelings discharged before any constructive program could be started. For the welfare
of the individual in trouble it was needful that this
clearing-away process should be done by someone
other than the person who finally carried through the
more positive program. Although the counselor cannot fail to recognize that someone else is getting credit
for what in part at least was his contribution, this must
not become in any degree discouraging. Doubtless he
will often find himself in the opposite situation, getting
a recognition that he realizes belongs in greater measure to someone who is receiving only criticism for not
having done better by the client.

In everything that the minister does as a counselor
there is sure to be some measure of suggestion. This is
inevitable because no one can come close to another
person's emotional difficulty without influencing him.
It is important that the minister frankly recognize this
and that he take great care not to overuse this opportunity of making an emotional transfer from himself
to the other individual. Since he wishes genuine and
lasting results, he will abstain from any magic-like use
of the resources of suggestion.

There can be no doubt about the danger that comes
from the fact that we are all susceptible to the suggestions of others. Because of this, much evil enters human
life. This, however, does not mean that the use of

suggestion is to be condemned but only that it demands great conscientiousness on the part of anyone consciously using his opportunity to influence someone else, a steadfast desire to strengthen rather than to weaken the character of the person making response. Suggestion plays such an important rôle in counseling that it deserves discussion in the following chapter on the art of counseling.

The Protestant minister occasionally will find that, whether he takes over domestic counseling or not, he must assume the priestly function in order to bring persons in great spiritual distress the assurance of forgiveness. The Protestant way of thinking considers forgiveness of sin an act of God through a relationship into which a third person has no right to intrude. Occasionally individuals come for help who have a burden of guilt which they can get rid of only by a certainty that they have been forgiven. This sense of forgiveness can only be achieved through a pronouncement spoken by someone who to them acts as a representative of God with the right to speak for Him. The same situation will sometimes arise in domestic counseling, and whatever the form of giving such an assurance, it must leave the client with the feeling that someone with authority has spoken for God Himself. It may well be that such individuals logically should be members of the Catholic Church since their need calls for the service of a person who has accepted the priestly rôle, but if their training has been Protestant and they are utterly unaware that they are diverging from the attitude of their own branch of Christianity, their release from a sense of sin must come through a mediator in whom they have confidence, and if the minister refuses to give them the needed assurance, they are left helpless with no way of escape. Nathaniel Hawthorne, who was skilled in the psycho-analytic probing of character many years before Freud, gave us in the *Marble Faun* an illustration of a Protestant in trouble who needed the spoken assurance which he found only through the Catholic confession. The domestic counselor may not be asked in words to assume the priestly function, but the spirit of confidence may prompt confession. This frankness will fail to bring relief and an incentive to a new beginning unless the client is left feeling that he is entirely and spiritually reinstated. He should not look in vain to the counselor for this assurance.

The counselor will often find that it is a great advantage to ask the client to write out his life history as fully as possible. As a rule, even though the latter may be reluctant at first to trace his life career, the effort will usually become interesting as it proceeds, and both relief and insight will come with the writing. It will also be an advantage to the counselor. This life history is likely to be more dependable in its emotional statements than the interview. It may also be especially valuable in revealing influences in the past that might not otherwise appear. It should be as individual and spontaneous as possible, and the counselor should avoid, therefore, giving any stereotyped questionnaire. It, of course, cannot be regarded as an accurate, objective description of facts but as a highly subjective disclosure which will certainly aid the counselor in understanding the inner life of thought and feeling belonging to the client.

These life histories will also become valuable parts of the record of the case. The counselor must make it clear to the conferee that this material, although filed, can never be identified by any other persons lest there be worry later on account of what has been committed to writing. The counselor, therefore, will remove the name and, in its place, write in a number or some identifying symbol that cannot be interpreted by anybody but himself. Care will be taken to explain this procedure to the client, even though he or she at the time expresses no concern.

CHAPTER IX

The Art of Domestic Counseling

ONE of the wonders of life is the way human faces differ. Although there is little to determine the appearance, chiefly mouth, teeth, lips, eyes, eyebrows, nose, cheek bone and chin, the effect of the combination of these features is that rarely do we have, except in twins, two persons who look much alike. The differences we find, when we look at the countenances of the persons passing along the street, are nothing less than amazing. There are even greater differences in the personalities of the men and women we meet, but we have no way of getting at this by looking at them. We have to have opportunity to be with them, to talk with them, and, as we say, to size them up. Sometimes we get a clear impression quickly; at other times it takes years to form an opinion and even then we have considerable uncertainty.

The first thing that a minister who attempts domestic counseling must not only intellectually realize but emotionally feel strongly is this unlikeness of people. Frequently it is the explanation of the problem brought to the counselor. Sometimes the understanding and accepting of this on the part of both husband and wife makes possible the solution of their difficulty. The greater significance of this fact of difference is the recognition of uniqueness that must be made whenever we attempt to deal helpfully with the difficulties of people. There can be for the counselor no mechanical routine, no scheme of classification, no automatic method of diagnosis which permits grouping people who have similar problems and giving them a stereotyped treatment. The individual has to be regarded as unduplicated even though the situation and problem he brings seem similar to those of others. Because he has a personality that belongs to no one else, his career cannot be duplicated and the real meaning of his problem is something that no one else has experienced.

It happens also that counseling, in order to be effective and helpful, has to get as close as possible to this underlying, highly individual root of the problem. Even if the conferee uses the same words as someone else in describing his situation, this merely means that words alone cannot carry the deeper distinctiveness. The peculiarity that marks off the experience of one as compared with any other consists largely of the emotional setting in which the problem is embedded. The individual has an emotional background that he alone possesses, and the reaction that he gives his problem is necessarily unlike that of any other. These differences may be great or small. We cannot, however, in counseling assume that they are trivial until we have made the best effort we can to find out the emotional meaning of the unique experience.

The first thing, therefore, that the domestic counselor has to learn is to keep his mind from its eagerness to classify people as the same in personality or in the nature of their problems. These differences are most subtle and of greater consequence for therapeutic counseling than those idiosyncrasies of organic causation which the physician has to keep in mind as he treats people for physical ills.

It is not easy always to see individuals as unique personalities. We are prone to bunch people together and to tag them with the same description because this is a comfortable way of thinking about them and dealing with them. Unless the counselor disciplines himself and learns the art of seeing every human being as a personality separated from all others, he will find himself lumping together men and women who are only superficially, in the externals of their situation, alike. Whether the minister is more tempted than other people to classify types and therefore has to overcome this professional handicap, who can say? It is as fallacious to tag members of any profession with a certain characteristic as it is to make any other kind of group generalization. It may be well, however, for the minister to face the fact that in his kind of service it is very easy to get the habit of grouping people largely according to a moral scheme of classification that he develops because of his special interest in people. Morals and religious attitudes mean so much to him that he may fall into a routine of separating people by his interpretation of their moral or religious characteristics. If he gets this habit it will make him an unsafe counselor. He will make premature judgments and allow them too greatly to influence his counseling procedure. He is liable to form conclusions as to the cause of the problem and the course that the conferee should take, before he has explored more than the frontier of the personal life which it is his business to understand. Such counseling is not reacting to the realities of the life situation presented, but rather to preconceived attitudes which burst into verbal expression whenever they are awakened by facts or circumstances to which the minister responds according to a well-developed habit.

As a result of his professional interest, the minister has an asset that should help him to keep his counseling individual. He is more interested in the personality welfare of the people with whom he has contact than is true of the members of most professions. The doctor has a similar interest, but it is largely confined to body welfare. The business man, lawyer, politician and engineer are more concerned with external accomplishments than with the inner meaning of these to the persons with whom they deal professionally. The aspect of the man or woman for which the minister has chief concern is that inner life which is the very heart of the personality which the counselor needs most to know. Therefore, the minister who seeks for this trait but does not attempt to read into the situation his own personal reactions has made the right start as a domestic counselor.

It is important to notice what the undisciplined counselor is apt to make himself the basis of his classifying and comparing of people. Unconsciously, that is, without realizing what he does, he is prone to establish himself as the standard. In the psychiatric meaning of unconsciousness, this use of the self is likely also to be influenced by feelings and motivations which he hides from himself. A minister recently broke the engagement of his daughter through constant criticism of certain faults in the young man. The result of this was the nervous breakdown of the young woman. Her partial recovery came after receiving expert analysis and treatment at a sanatorium. The specialist felt, however, that there was a portion of this problem that needed to be handled by a domestic counselor. In rehearsing her experience, the young woman revealed an intense hostility to her father, remarking upon the strange fact that the faults which the young man had, about which her father had talked continuously, were exactly the chief flaws of his own character. This is a good illustration of the dangers that come from the counselor's being himself in conflict or having feelings or desires against which he has built an emotional barricade.

The counselor is tempted not only to make his personality the standard by which he measures all men, but to use every opportunity of counseling as a means of strengthening the fortification which he has erected against self-criticism. He will therefore read into other people motives that originate from himself and this he will do without realizing how his own emotional reaction is distorting the problem he is attempting to interpret.

Whether any one of us can completely objectify

our career is something about which thoughtful persons may disagree. The psychiatrist may claim the achievement of this high level, but the minister has need of being more modest. It is surely wrong to tell him that he cannot counsel until he is certain that he has freed himself from every subjective influence. He is expected to be a pastor, and counseling is becoming more and more a necessary part of this aspect of his work. If insistence is made upon his ridding himself of any tendency to see others through his own self-life, the result will be that those who are most thoroughly at the mercy of unconscious motivation will alone feel equal to the task, while the more self-understanding and sensitive, and therefore better equipped, will hesitate to accept a responsibility for which they think they are not psychically prepared.

The important thing is that the minister understand the need of being objective, the danger of letting his personal experiences and outlook upon life discolor whatever is said to him during a conference. If he puts himself on guard against this very natural human inclination, he is building a habit of mind that justifies his counseling, and one that will increasingly make it trustworthy.

It will help immeasurably if he can cultivate sympathy for others and interest in their experience, if he can gain the attitude of mind that leads the novelist to write books. His interest, however, will be in flesh and blood people. Often he will discover that fact is indeed more extraordinary and dramatic than fiction. He will learn the delight of delving in character, not

from a hardhearted curiosity, but from a kindly eagerness to make life easier for people in trouble. The
essential thing is to get the minister started on this
special kind of exploring. Once it begins, the interest
that it brings will provide the means of growth. It is
like any other form of investigation or exploration.
Once embarked upon, it becomes intensely fascinating.
Indeed, the time may come when the minister will
need to hold it in check, chiefly expressing it in the
hours given to counseling, because its appeal will become so great that it will tend to possess too large a
part of his interest.

The young minister who wishes to strengthen his
objective attitudes toward people will find the reading
of case histories and psychological and psychiatric
analyses helpful if only he keeps himself catholic-
minded and does not, in an amateur fashion, become
the disciple of some special school of interpretation.
The novelist will also contribute if his books are
pondered and an effort is made to trace the causation
portrayed and carry it back into the nature of the personality out of which it comes. The minister will need,
however, to develop a more critical, analyzing habit
of mind than the usual reader of fiction possesses.
This will bring him into fellowship with the author
who, as a rule, has chosen his life work because of his
desire to create characters from his knowledge of
human nature. The minister will also encourage his
own sympathy and increase his insight by removing
his interest as often as possible outside himself and
tying it up with the people with whom he associates.

He will begin to see men and women as individuals, the one thing most necessary for understanding them. This attitude is in many ways the rarest habit of people in their association with others. Even keen observers are likely to study others and find how to handle them and how to use them for personal advantage, rather than knowing them thoroughly because of a genuine interest in the make-up of their personality.

The minister can apply to his preaching much of this interest in the dramatic and tragic happenings of human life. Both the Old and the New Testaments are filled with personality characterization, and the portrayal of this can be made effective in its appeal and at the same time become the means of encouraging in the minister the habit of looking into people objectively and finding the true content of their personalities. The material, however, must be transformed into the form belonging to the sermon, for if it becomes a rehearsal of case history or anything that approaches the manner of the counselor's analysis it is sure to seem out of place and to turn aside the interest of the hearers. The study of the presentation of some of our most famous preachers and evangelists from Wesley and Whitefield to our own time will help in learning to give the incisive, dramatic uncovering of character traits that has often been the most effective element in the great preaching of the past. Great differences will be found in the method of doing this, ranging from the concreteness of D. L. Moody to the more generalized illustrations of Phillips Brooks, but an objective trait will be found in all who have made good use in their speaking of their knowledge of human character.

As a rule, anyone who comes to the domestic counselor for help is concerned with a definite problem. Sometimes it is recognized that this has several phases, but more often the conferee expects that the discussion will be related to one specific matter. It is rarely true, however, that the domestic counselor can safely restrict himself to the consideration of the difficulty as it is presented. He finds himself in the position of the doctor when a patient comes asking that something be done to take away a headache. Possibly the physician could easily accomplish this and satisfy his client but it would be contrary to good medical practice. He realizes that what is important is that he discover, if possible, what causes the headache, since that, instead of the suffering itself, is what needs treatment. If the counselor were willing to give to the man or woman who is asking help the privilege of deciding what should be discussed, it would mean that the analysis of the case would be made not by the counselor but by the counselee. To allow this to happen would destroy the purpose of the conference.

The question, therefore, always arises, how far the topic about which the conferee wishes to talk should be discussed, since the responsibility of deciding this must remain with the counselor. There are two important facts that he always has to consider. One is that no problem can possibly be detached from the character of the person. The great bulk of the meaning of any problem must be found in the personality and in the experiences the individual has had. Although this is true, it is equally obvious that domestic counseling has a function quite different from that belonging to the psychoanalyst. If the significance is great enough to require a thorough searching of the personality in all its aspects, it is a case that belongs to the psychiatrist, and the only thing that a domestic counselor can safely do is to direct the client to someone who is professionally prepared to handle it. On the other hand, it must be remembered that the psychiatrists cannot possibly take under their charge every sort of social difficulty. There are not enough psychiatrists to do this. Indeed, it would mean in many cases that they must neglect work that they should do, in order to carry on what can better be done by persons who do not have such a serious analytic interest.

When the counselor has decided that the problem presented to him is not one that should be farmed out to the psychiatrist, the question still remains, how much of past history, how much insight regarding the inheritance, the disposition, and the career of the individual needs to be discovered as a means of helping him with his problem. The answer must be that what seems pertinent should be uncovered for the purpose of gathering insight both as to the meaning of the problem and as to the character and the resources of the man or woman.

If it is felt that more is required, that processes need to be started to reconstruct his life, it is highly questionable whether the domestic counselor can safely attempt such a serious program. He is embarking upon a course that challenges the skill of the psychiatrist who dares not attempt such a function unless he has had long-continued coöperation and the opportunity to plow up the history of the individual in a thorough-going way denied to the counselor even if he has had proper professional training for undertaking the task. It is clear, however, that the counselor will seldom be content to limit himself to the mere surface appearance of a problem which he knows comes out of the personality and which can only be solved by achieving a considerable knowledge of the characteristics of the personality.

In addition to the fact that the great bulk of the meaning of any problem lies outside itself, there is something else that the counselor must also keep in mind. His searching for information must have as its purpose the helping of the individual. He is not delving into character formation primarily as an investigator, but is assuming the rôle of therapeutic service. It is frequently within his power to dig up the past in such a way as to increase the emotional tension, for which there can be no relief unless there be a more thorough analysis than it is the right of the counselor to make. This gives the counselor a clue as to his procedure and one that is especially important for the minister. Unless the minister is willing to abandon his position and assume the prerogatives of a different profession, he must be content in dealing with people to concern himself with the problem presented and with its more apparent sources, rather than to attempt the thorough upheaval of character causation that for more serious purposes is the proper procedure of the psychiatrist and the psychoanalyst.

In the rapport that is established between the counselor and counselee, and the emotional sensitivity of the counselor to the other, is found the clue to the procedure during the conference. The interest the counselor takes in the background of the problem presented results not from the desire to unravel as fully as possible the causations represented, but rather to discover how to handle the problem that has been brought him. Although this is the main center of interest, the concentration is not narrowed to the point where no insight as to its meaning is sought in the previous history and in the disposition of the individual. The counselor must not be led astray and become fascinated in the tracing of character for its own sake. Instead, the need of the conferee must always continue as the central interest.

The minister cannot expect to make use of the elaborate testing of the personality that is possible for the psychologist in his laboratory or for the psychiatrist through a long-continued analysis. If the minister is to function as a domestic counselor under conditions that he can fulfill, he must recognize necessary limitations of time and resources, and if the problem requires more than he is free to carry through, either the client must be sent elsewhere or the counselor must obtain the coöperation of persons who can draw upon professional skill or resources that he does not possess.

At times it will become apparent to the minister that

before he accepts any responsibility in an attempt to deal with the problem presented, the man or woman should have a good physical examination. The need of this will usually be suggested by the nature of the problem or the condition of the counselee. It would be foolish always to insist upon such an examination since sometimes there are requests for information or for other types of service that indicate no necessity for first discovering the possibility of the influence of physical conditions.

But if there is any doubt whatsoever, the minister will find it a wise procedure to require a physical examination before he undertakes to give counsel. The fact that he does not have a medical background should make him more cautious lest he attempt to handle, on the psychic and social level, difficulties that have their origin in bodily ill health.

Some years ago a husband asked me to meet with him and with a psychiatrist who was trying to straighten out what was interpreted as domestic incompatibility. The husband said that his wife, who was being treated, had become jealous of his work, refusing to grow up emotionally, and the psychiatrist wanted to talk the case over with me because his program apparently had failed. Upon meeting with the two men and listening to the story, I was led to ask, first of all, whether the woman was physically well. I had met her once and, although I had had a mere casual contact, she had given me the impression of a wholesome type of personality. It was, therefore, hard for me to believe that she was emotionally so retarded

as suddenly, after years of marriage, to become jealous
of her husband's career. The psychiatrist assured me
that there was no physical trouble whatsoever. He had
examined her. I realized that this was not the proper
function of the psychiatrist, but since he was of course
medically trained I accepted his verdict. I suggested
that the husband and wife go on a vacation together,
hoping that the removal from the environment that
appeared to cause tension would give the man and
woman an opportunity to renew their one-time good
adjustment.

My counsel was followed and they went to a resort
city on the coast. Two or three days after their arrival
the wife was taken seriously ill. She was taken to one
of the best known of American hospitals near by
where it was found that it was necessary to have an
operation. It was started but never finished because,
as soon as the body was entered, it was found that the
woman was suffering from an enormous mass of
cancer, and that her situation was hopeless. She died
two days later. To me it has always seemed one of the
greatest tragedies I have known. This woman, after
having had a rich domestic fellowship for years, spent
the last months of her life trying to convince herself
that she was guilty of what were described as infantile
reactions. There can be no doubt that if there had
been normal suspicion of her physical condition,
justified by the fact that her disposition had apparently
changed so suddenly, a competent physical examination would have been made a prerequisite to the psychiatric treatment. Such an examination most surely

in this case would have discovered the cancerous condition.

The minister cannot afford to run risks. He must always be on guard lest the moral or social problem be merely an expression of an underlying physical or psychic malady that requires a different kind of ministration from what any clergyman is prepared to give. He should, of course, be exceptionally quick to notice the possible significance of any sudden change of disposition or behavior. With very few exceptions, men and women do not switch from the track along which their personalities have been moving, unless there be some fundamental change of disposition which is most apt to come from causations belonging to the territory of the physician or the psychiatrist. Even when there is no suspicion of any grave disability, it is a wise procedure to insist that the person have a physical examination and treatment of minor handicaps if necessary, in order that there may be the greatest quantity of energy possible for the meeting of the problem.

The domestic counselor needs to keep a list of physicians whom he can recommend, who are in sympathy with this preventive service. It will not be a wise policy, if it can be avoided, to have only one or two doctors to suggest to those coming for help, who need first of all to have a physical examination. On the other hand, the counselor does have a responsibility which cannot be met by refusing to make any recommendations. Usually he can advise that the man or woman see the family physician. In some instances, however, this policy will not be feasible. The counselee may not have a family physician, or the nature of the problem may suggest the need of an examination which the family physician is probably not well prepared to give. Good judgment is required in recommending specialists. I have found it an advantage to know the special interests, for example, of different psychiatrists practicing in a city where I have done considerable counseling. Knowing the kind of problem with which the specialist is most familiar gives a clue in many instances as to whom the conferee had better consult.

If the examiner advises treatment for some deficiency or malady that is discovered, the question whether the counselor should go on with his part or not, had better be left to the physician who has charge of the medical treatment. It may be an advantage for the counselor to make his contribution, or it may be necessary instead that he wait until the patient is better prepared, or it may seem likely that when greater health has been brought about the original problem will fade out of sight.

Some specialists are accused of being reluctant to drop a case that belongs not to them but to someone else. Probably such criticism is rarely deserved. The minister, however, can have no motive other than vanity for wishing to keep the therapeutic program in his own hands. His interest is only in helping the individual out of difficulty. Counseling is not his professional means of livelihood but a part of his pastoral responsibility. He has no professional reputation to nurse, and any reluctance on his part to send conferees to persons in other professions for needed services would be unpardonable. It must be kept in mind also that the necessity of sending the client to others may not appear at first but may arise in the process of counseling.

The domestic counselor cannot safely attempt to follow a set procedure, a professional technique, because this is prevented by the necessity of adapting the consultation to each individual situation. There is, however, an obligation that he assumes by his willingness to receive the client, and his ability to accomplish the task placed upon him gives him his credentials. He must have the willingness and the skill to enter the other's feelings. The first question which he must try to answer, even to become a helpful listener, is: "How does this person before me feel?" And then, "If I felt as he does, how would I conceive of the situation that had led me to seek counsel?"

We all realize at times how much we are shut away from other people, how little we know of their inner life, and how little they know of ours. In counseling, this chasm which separates each person from all others has to be crossed. It may well be said that we fly over this by the wings of sympathy. No other word comes so near to revealing what has to be done in entering another's life. It is literally a suffering with another. The counselor must be the kind of person who can do this more quickly and fully than people usually do in their associations with others. Unless one has a natural gift for such sympathy or can learn to make it an emotional habit, he had better steer clear of domestic counseling.

The reason why sympathy comes first is that the counselor cannot expect to deal with something he does not understand, and the something which he is seeking to apprehend is the way the other person sees his situation. To the counselee it is something definite, something not to be doubted, and of terrific importance. His thinking and feelings are so fixed upon it that he, for the moment, can see nothing else. Probably no one else would picture the condition as he does. It is, therefore, not an impersonal, accurate, objective portrayal of circumstances, as they would seem to a person of neutral-minded good judgment, but rather just what the man or woman in trouble believes to be true. This picture, faulty as it may be, because of the feeling it has generated, is the fact that has to be tackled. It must be accepted at first as the reality, even though in the end the counselor is able to reconstruct it for the other, or to show that it is an exaggerated or a false portrayal. Before one attempts to judge what is being said, this first expression of sympathy must be achieved. We must feel as the other feels. We must see things as he sees them. We must accept his interpretation of the problem he faces.

We are not, however, greatly interested in his effort to describe his difficulties as he tries intellectually to interpret them for us or to convince us so that he enlists our support. It is the feelings behind his words that are our first concern. We, therefore, for the moment abandon our analytic or judicial practices and try as nearly as we can to *be* the other person. We move into his life by close observation, through familiarity with the motivations and reactions that human beings share, and especially by catching the emotional meaning of everything the counselee says or does.

Our approach is diametrically opposite to that of the scrutinizing person who starts out trying to size up the individual and discover the objective facts of his situation. If we were to commence our counseling in this spirit we would remain aliens to the other's inmost worry, perplexity, or suffering and would, therefore, never know the nature of the problem with which we are concerned. We cannot function if we assume the rôle of the judge or deal with the situation as does the chemist when he makes an analysis of something which he is seeking to break up into its parts. It is a human being that concerns us. If we cannot gather any insight as to how he feels and thinks, any counsel on our part may miss the point absolutely and hence prove mischievous.

It is not, therefore, in a testing mood that we start our counseling. Instead we endeavor to bring ourselves, by sympathizing, into the emotion of the other. As much as possible we vicariously feel ourselves living the other person's life.

Not only by our sympathy do we approach an understanding of the other's conception and emotional reaction to it, but by our effort we also establish a rapport which makes it possible for us to carry through our later responsibilities as a counselor with some hope of accomplishment. The person in trouble soon ceases to feel the self-consciousness, the necessity of demonstrating himself, to have the readiness to react with

sensitiveness or anger or some other emotional out-
burst, any one of which may have been at the bursting-
out point when he first found himself face to face with
the interviewer. Instead of the critic or judge or un-
feeling analyst against whom he had guarded himself,
he discovers the person that he may have thought did
not exist, a friendly person whom he can tell just how
he feels and what he thinks to be true. The emotional
alliance insures the rapport without which the counselor cannot function.

The emotional quality of his entrance into the life
of another human being protects the counselor from
assuming a position of superiority. Anyone in trouble
who comes to another for help is exceedingly sensitive
to any attitude that lessens his self-esteem. He is emotionally in readiness to detect any assumption of authority over him, since almost always there is in some
measure an underlying feeling of inferiority. There is
always the temptation, when one attempts to help another, to use the latter's weakness to build up one's
own feeling of superiority. That this reaction is not
uncommon in the physician's attitude toward his
patient was made clear some years ago by one of
America's greatest psychiatrists, William A. White.[1]
He showed how detrimental this rôle of superiority
was as an obstacle to the physician's attempt at treating
the sick person. It is a much more abnormal intrusion
of self-regard when it appears in domestic counseling
than when it appears in the doctor's attitude toward

---

[1] "The Dynamics of the Relation of Physician and Patient,"
Mental Hygiene, Vol. X, No. 1, pp. 1–11.

his patient. We can accept in physical illness what becomes intolerable when we are struggling with a social situation.

The minister, by his calling, should be not only exceptionally prepared for the sympathy necessary to enter another person's feelings; he should also be better protected than most men against any assumption of superiority. His sense of spiritual values, his realization of human weakness, naturally turn him away from any self-exploiting as he wrestles with other people's troubles. It only behooves him to carry to any domestic counseling the same spirit of friendliness and self-forgetfulness that people generally assume to be a character trait that befits him for his high calling.

The domestic counselor who has successfully detached himself from his own prejudices and self-regard that he may come close to the human being who has need of him, naturally makes an individual approach to the problem presented. It is not that he avoids any stereotyped procedure because he knows that this would defeat his purposes. It is rather that he has become so thoroughly identified with the other person that it is most natural for him to adapt himself to the particular personality now in his presence.

Nothing could be more mischievous than to suggest that there is one proper way to start the interview. It would not be wise, even as an automatic first step, to invite the conferee to sit down. He may not be at the moment in the mood to seat himself, and any effort to force this may break into his concentration of emotion and make him self-conscious. Even so simple an act of courtesy cannot be made a stereotyped beginning. It may be much wiser for the counselor to stand up himself and even to walk back and forth if that is what the other is doing. This sharing of emotion, insignificant as it may seem, will help the fusion of personalities, the importance of which has already been emphasized.

The calmness that is needed may come all the sooner if nothing is done to force the conferee to act contrary to the mood in which he temporarily finds himself. Rarely, of course, would it be out of order to ask the conferee to make himself comfortable in a chair. This is, however, a good illustration of the fact that nothing must be assumed as an inevitable procedure but rather that, from the beginning to the end, the conference of counselor and counselee must be as individual as the problem itself.

It is usually not long before the conferee makes clear his expectation. He has come for a purpose and as soon as he finds himself in good rapport or has sufficiently relieved himself of strong feeling, he discloses what he desires. Since, as we have seen, the expectations necessarily look toward the future, it is of the utmost importance, especially because of the revelation of character it brings, that the counselor discover the basic desire even though it be entangled with a great amount of emotionalism or extraneous details.

Unfortunately, the counselor cannot at this time accept without scrutiny what the conferee puts into words. Experience teaches us that the real purpose, the deep-seated desire, is frequently concealed from the mind of the person in trouble or is deliberately covered up in the effort to win sympathy without admitting frankly the wishes that, it is feared, will bring criticism. The conferee may even go so far as to express sentiments and desires that are exactly opposite to what actually exist.

The counselor, being aware of this possibility of self-deception or of willful falsifying, is on his guard. He realizes that he must get some clue as to what are the real purposes of the man or woman who is asking help. If this is not revealed by the words that are spoken or the strength of the feeling that is expressed, it is likely sooner or later to appear in statements, exclamations or even facial expressions that suggest the true motivations of the person in trouble, thus giving the counselor an opportunity, by questioning, to get at the facts he has to know. The individual who is trying to conceal, or who is driven by some desire or feeling that he is repressing, is in a state of tension which leads him to say or do things which the observing person is quick to detect. By further questioning, the counselor can then use the insight he has gained as a starting point for a more honest and factual presentation.

The counselor, as soon as he has the clue he needs in his grasp, finds himself turning away from his preliminary sympathy toward a more critical, analyzing attitude of mind. It was well for him to enter the other person's feelings, but he cannot be of any help if he remains merely an emotional ally. His sympathy was a means of getting at the realities that he had to know in order to carry through the judicial thinking that is now in order.

This reversal of the counselor's attitude is not so difficult as it might seem. It is natural for all of us, when our sympathy has been aroused, sooner or later to ponder over what we have seen or heard. The domestic counselor merely starts this process sooner than we do in our usual contacts with people. Since he realizes that he must form a judgment free from the feelings of the persons in trouble, this scrutinizing soon becomes a habit. Once it starts, there is a double process of thinking; the hearer listens to what is said and tries to get its meaning, including its emotional content, while at the same time attempting to see the situation objectively, so as to get the insight that permits eventually the giving of counsel. This thinking along two fronts is not infrequent in life, since to some extent we nearly always do this when we listen intently to any revelation that is being made. The counselor merely does it more thoroughly than is usually true.

Assuming that the counselor meets these requirements that are prerequisite to his proper service, it is now in order to discuss the various ways in which he may function. In many cases, it soon appears that the client must be led to a self-discovery that is necessary if he is to handle his problem. Since it is not likely to prove effective, the counselor does not try to bring about this disclosure, himself, by pointedly stating to the other the facts that ought to be recognized. Instead, in a more subtle fashion, he asks questions or makes comments and gradually melts away the false assumption, or the self-protection, or the wrong interpretations that are misleading the conferee.

Sometimes it seems more helpful to do this quickly and harshly, but, as a rule, the procedure is just the contrary. In these, the majority of cases, it would be most unwise to try to force the necessary self-understanding. It can best come gently and gradually, in order that there may not be any emotional resentment.

The counselor keeps in mind that he is not concerned with having the other individual get the true picture of himself merely that he may have a self-portrayal that is accurate, but rather because unless this trustworthy insight is gathered, the problem cannot dissolve. It is, therefore, not the business of the counselor to force self-knowledge, but rather to lead the client out of difficulties that are themselves, at least in great measure, the consequences of his own personal choices and attitudes.

If it seems a hopeless task to help another to self-discovery, it is well to keep in mind that the client has come because he is in trouble and wishes to get out of his uncomfortable situation. His need of help gives a promise to the effort of the counselor that would not otherwise exist. Even though the conferee may be reluctant to look at himself honestly and may much prefer some other method of solving his problem, he is nevertheless under pressure and not inclined to antagonize any effort to help him, if nothing is done in a way to stir up unnecessarily his hostility by destroying his self-respect.

Again, the pragmatic character of the counselor's service must not be forgotten. There is not the time, nor, on the part of the counselor, the professional training that is necessary for a thorough self-inspection. The minister is not asked to do the same sort of task that rightly belongs to the psychoanalyst. He is seeking to develop the self-knowledge that is required for the solution of the definite problem presented. If this cannot be accomplished without going still farther, it becomes clear that the client should be advised to go elsewhere for a more skillful and more detailed analytic service.

The counselor is seeking to have the man or woman who has come to him gather the self-interpretation that dealing with the problem demands. This influences the procedure of the counselor. He injects questions or comments that are related to what the client is saying about his problem but that also encourage the latter to think about the meaning of what he is saying as it applies to himself. In spite of his emotional defenses he can hardly avoid catching the drift of the counselor's queries and suggestions. The counselor's questioning must never be made to seem an attack on the client's personality, but rather an attempt to get at the significance of the problem. If the sympathy of the counselor had not already been recognized, the reaction might be an increasing feeling of opposition, finally reaching the point where the client would become so antagonistic that counseling could not continue with any hope of success.

As the preceding chapter has pointed out, the counselor is sometimes given the rôle of an interpreter if the client comes chiefly asking for nonpartisan, objective insight. When this is true, the process of self-discovery can, as a rule, proceed more rapidly. The client has already assumed an unemotional attitude toward himself, since if this were not true he would not be asking someone else to describe the situation as it seems to him. It may be, of course, that this request for an objective judgment may not be honest, but merely an attempt to win an advocate. The counselor, however, will not be taken in by mere words but will test the sincerity of the individual and as a result may sometimes be convinced that, first of all, he must try to get through the fallacious ideas that the client has gathered to protect himself against self-knowledge.

The counselor will do his utmost to prevent the individual seeking help from becoming emotional regarding himself and attempting to heap the blame upon himself and thereby create guilt. This self-punishment is as liable under the circumstances as is self-deception. It brings no advantage to change the latter to the former since the counselor is asking for an unemotional, intelligent handling of the problem. To be dominated by one emotion is as hazardous as to be controlled by the other.

The counselor will not always be greatly concerned about developing self-knowledge. It all depends upon the type of problem presented. Even when better understanding of self might be an advantage, it may not be of major concern in the solution of the problem.

Sometimes it appears that the counselor must concentrate upon helping the conferee come to a self-decision. The need of this may already be more or less realized by the man or woman, who finds it difficult to do what clearly should be done. It happens, therefore, that the counselor's task may be clearly that of leading to a final settlement or it may be rather that he must help the person in trouble to see the nature of the decision to be made, and then encourage him to carry out his conviction.

The discovery of the needed decision or the willingness to carry it out may be obstructed by very strong feeling. It would, therefore, be useless for the counselor merely to listen to the statement of the person in trouble, and then give his decision as to what must be done, in the way that the physician writes out a prescription. In domestic counseling the integrity of the individual must be maintained. It is necessary, therefore, to lead the one who has to make a difficult decision to see for himself the reasons why he must act. The consequence of this is that the counselor again has to carry on his part, asking questions and making suggestions, in such a way that the emotion which is preventing the proper decision is pushed aside at least to such a degree that intelligence can function.

The domestic counselor is not surprised when there is a great outpouring of emotion during the conference. He does not think of this as a mere relief, something associated with the client's reaction to his circumstances, which must be patiently accepted, but instead he sees its therapeutic value. Frequently, the counselor himself comes to feel that one of his greatest services is to encourage this free expression of feeling that frequently has been long concealed, since it must somehow be gotten out of the individual's inner life or there is no opportunity for judgment to function. The counselor, therefore, even when his objective soon appears to be that of leading the conferee to make for himself the judgment that any unprejudiced person of experience would see is required, should not try to hasten the process of self-knowledge and quickly get the client ready to do what eventually is necessary if any headway is to be made with the problem. Instead, the relief of feeling, even of prejudice, is encouraged. It usually needs little outside stimulus, but merely a listener who seems near in sympathy and who is known to keep confidences.

At times the counselor will feel an obligation to give support to the person who has come to see that a decision ought to be made, but who seems to lack the will to come to the point. It is folly to deny that suggestion functions in such a situation. The counselor has used suggestion in helping his client to see what should be done. It is not improper to recognize this and to direct one's influence toward the necessary settlement. The counselor, however, should beware of going so far as to let the conferee turn over the deciding to the counselor.

We do not have the moral right thus to determine the career of another and, if we are wise counselors, we see that the decision, to be successful, must be the genuine commitment of the person in trouble. He must go away finally not only to do what he should, but to do it with conviction and with the belief that he himself has made the decision. It will do him no harm to feel that he has been helped to see the need of it through his conference. He realizes that this is what he had a right to expect to come out of the conference. If, however, he goes away to attempt faintheartedly to carry out what he still does not really wish to do, or is not fully persuaded he should do, little good has been accomplished.

In this attempt to help another discover a decision which he should make, the counselor can, of course, follow no set procedure. Here, as in all other counseling service, there must be the facility to adapt to the personality and the circumstances of a particular case. The minister should be favored in this effort by the fact that he is, by his calling, inclined to recognize individuality. He can hardly succeed even in his preaching, much less in his pastoral work, unless he trains himself to see people as persons and to react sensitively to their uniqueness. The more he acts as a domestic counselor, the more impressed he is with the fact that he is not called upon to treat problems nor to deal with a situation, but rather to help an individual who is wrestling with a problem that draws much of its meaning from the character of the personality facing it.

The art of counseling, therefore, is not the process of abstracting the problem and clarifying it nor of disclosing the decision it requires, but rather the help-ing of the personality involved. The counseling process, therefore, is something more than the phy-sician's effort at diagnosis. It is in itself an attempt, through adaptation to the individual, to strengthen or reconstruct his inner emotional life so that he can carry out the adjustment required.

Sometimes the counselor soon discovers in the process of the conference that he must help the client to delay the decision rather than to follow his inclina-tion to act impulsively. In an instance of this sort the client becomes fully convinced that he knows just what his problem is, and what should be done, and all he wants is some assistance in working out a program he has determined to put through. The counselor has the same task of lessening emotion as in the former type of consultation, but the purpose has changed. He now sees that he should help the client realize either that he is not in the mood to make the final decision or that the time is not yet ripe for it. It will frequently be found that, when shocked by a sudden discovery of her husband's misdoings, a wife through strong feeling, will be determined upon getting a divorce. Her emotion runs too high to give her any opportunity to look forward to the consequences that must follow the decision. Her divorce may involve the welfare of children. It may prevent reconciliation that to the counselor seems hopeless only because of the strength of the wife's feelings. He has learned from experience that such feelings frequently disappear once the divorce is carried through and are replaced by regret and even by dismay. Even when the counselor's judgment agrees with that of his client, he may wish to delay action because the emotional attitude associated with getting a divorce may make the consequences more distressing, more harmful than if the same decision were carried out in a more normal frame of mind.

He may, on the other hand, see clearly that his obligation is to save the conferee, who is beside himself, from doing something that he will probably not wish to do if only there can be sufficient delay to allow the action of intelligence. Just how he is to make this plain and persuasive will again depend upon the individual situation. It will mean throwing away words to attempt the giving of advice. There must be a more subtle undermining of the emotional mood, a draining away of the intensity of feeling. Again, questions must be asked and comments made that will gradually prepare the client to be told or to discover for himself the value of delaying any overt act. Sometimes it will be found expedient to insist upon several consultations. The counselor will be playing for time because he has come to understand what an effective ally this can be to one who is beside himself because of the tyranny of sudden shock.

The motive behind the course that has been settled upon is frequently vengeance. One has been hurt and, therefore, wishes to pay back the injury. The mind so concentrates upon this satisfaction that nothing else enters consciousness. Hate, however strong, cannot become, except possibly in the case of a few psycho-

pathic persons, an abiding motivation. Once pain has
been inflicted, the hatred immediately disappears. This
is the theme of Browning's poems, "Before" and
"After." We are all familiar with the ease with which
this transformation takes place.

It follows, therefore, that any decision made because
of hate or the desire for revenge is a catering to the
emotion felt by the person in trouble and cannot be a
solution for the problem which eventually he must
face. Since the counselor is not tied up with a similar
emotionalism, he quickly realizes how unready his
client is to make any decision that will have influence
in the final settlement of the problem. The excursion
he vicariously has made into the life of the other person has led him to see how coercive the resentment
or the craving for vengeance is. Since he is also capable
of objectively surveying the situation, he realizes the
great distance between the emotional reaction and any
intelligent analysis of facts, and is certain that in time
this will be recognized as clearly by the client as it is
at present by himself. However much a man or woman
has suffered from the misdoings of somebody else, he
is in the mood to hurt himself even more seriously
through eagerness to act upon emotions that, although
in command, are far distant from the normal feelings
that later are sure to assert themselves.

How can the conferee be saved from a decision
that agrees with the temporary flooding of emotion
and runs counter to the calmer, characteristic feeling
which eventually takes possession and determines
values, day by day? That is the difficult question that

faces the domestic counselor. It may seem to him that
he can do no more at the moment than to delay any
carrying out of the decision that has already been
made. The stronger the emotion expressed at the time,
the more the counselor will suspect it, since its very
intensity is likely to force reaction.

Nothing would be more mischievous than for the
minister, giving domestic counsel, to be himself captivated by what he is told, so that his emotion also
becomes coercive. He must always consider that in
most cases he is getting only one person's side and
that this is being presented with a discoloring that
strong feeling is likely to bring. Also, even if the counselor is hearing a faithful portrayal that makes his
fierce, moral reaction seem proper under the circumstances, he is as unfitted to direct the decision, while
emotionally involved, as is his client.

Several years ago a minister who had never seriously
thought about his responsibility as a domestic counselor had thrust upon him a family tragedy. He was a
well-meaning, conventional type of preacher, ill prepared to deal with a crisis with any degree of factual,
objective insight. A woman in his church, beside herself with anger and humiliation, reported that her
daughter was pregnant. She wanted the pastor to deal
with the young man responsible and force him to
marry her daughter. The minister was soon almost as
thoroughly stirred up as the mother. To him the problem was nothing other than a moral responsibility.
Calling the young man to his house, he announced,
without giving the young fellow any chance to speak,

that he must marry the girl whom he had made pregnant or go to jail.

It happened that the man was in love with the girl and had accepted his responsibility. Although it meant leaving college before graduating he had willingly decided to marry immediately and get a job. Since he knew, as later facts made clear, that the girl was even more responsible than himself, the assault made upon him before he was able to explain what he was willing to do angered him and completely changed his attitude toward the problem. He married the girl, but with a feeling that he had been unjustly treated, and with bitterness toward his wife's family.

A relative who learned about the situation just before the marriage took place came and asked me if there was anything that I could do at the eleventh hour that would give the young man and woman some chance of making a successful marriage. It was evident that it was too late and I could only tell this friend of the family later on that I did not believe the husband would stay long with his wife or that there was any hope of the marriage turning out well. My prophecy, unfortunately, proved true. Soon after the marriage, the young man announced that he had found a job in South America and packed up and disappeared. Later it was discovered that he was living in the United States, but he could not be induced to return to his wife. She obtained a divorce. Again she became pregnant before marriage and this time the situation was faced in a different spirit. The minister was not invited to contribute to the solution. This woman has now been married some years and has apparently become a happy, well-adjusted wife and also, as it may surprise some readers to know, a faithful spouse.

The great majority of domestic conferences bring to the counselor a task that is as important as it is difficult. He must help the man or woman, who has brought a grievance, to become detached from self-concern and get some inkling of the feelings and convictions of the other person. It is rare that all trouble-making is on one side. Frequently a man or woman knows and frankly states this, admitting that he or she is not flawless, and that the other spouse has a right to find fault. However, this is usually a mere verbal statement. It is accepted in consciousness as a generalization but has little content. It is expressed because such apparent frankness in itself strengthens the case the client wishes to present to the counselor.

It is the latter's task to put meaning into this admission, although usually the person in trouble has organized his thinking and feeling to protect himself from accepting responsibility for the situation that has arisen. This crust of self-defense the counselor must penetrate and, again, his instruments are questions and comments. It is generally apparent that there cannot be any direct path, but rather that he must succeed in turning the flank of the individual's self-justification. The counselor does not expect to accomplish his purpose quickly, but if he is persistent and willing to make slow progress he is likely in the end to bring to the client some realization of the situation of the other person involved.

The counselor does not seek to bring this about in order that he can get his client to accept part of the blame. He will take care to keep that word out of the discussion and as far as possible to lessen the inclination, always present in a conflict between persons, to place responsibility. The counselor is not trying a case, but seeking to solve a problem.

Even if separation or divorce is the only way out, there is still need of having the solution face forward, rather than toward the past. The reason why the counselor wishes to develop in the conferee a measure of other-regard is that no program can be satisfactory that is emotionally tied up with a false conception of the total situation. Whatever decision may be made regarding the immediate problem, there remains the necessity of developing a life program. A decision must, of course, eventually be made concerning the immediate issue, but what is more important is that a foundation be laid for a stronger and more wholesome personality. There is little hope of this being true if the individual is left with the luxury of self-pity, drawn from seeing one side of a situation to which two people have contributed.

The minister should be the last person to forget that a good use of mistakes, committed in the past, is to force them to contribute to a greater maturity and insight. It is not possible, however, to learn the lesson of one's blunders and sufferings if they are misinterpreted through self-deception.

Thus the domestic counselor comes to see that it is his function not only to lead people toward right decisions but also that it is his opportunity, as he gives his counsel, to encourage the building of character. He will not resort to preachment but rather will attempt to use the occasion as a means of reëducation. In any case the conferee will be left weaker or stronger as a result of the experience, and it is the task of the minister to see that it is the latter rather than the former.

Since the domestic counselor learns that anything can happen, he is not surprised occasionally to find that he must encourage the self-interest of the conferee who is in danger of being exploited by the intense sympathy felt for the other person involved in the problem. The wife or husband may be in the mood to take all the blame, and it may be this tendency which has wrecked the domestic compatibility. Just as persons may be too generous for their own good or for the welfare of those whom they love, so also a person may be so concerned with the feelings and desires of someone else as to wreck comradeship. Persons who have already ruined happiness by self-effacement come seeking help and pour out the mistakes they have made, trouble for which they feel responsible, without realizing that their chief error has been a self-suppression which can be as deadly in fellowship as unmitigated self-regard. What would be a generous spirit, were it not so exaggerated and self-diminishing, becomes the source of chronic irritation and frustration.

The domestic counselor finds this fault of too much concern for others a far more difficult life pattern to

change than that of too much self-regard. The practice is supported by the conviction that it is an evidence of unselfishness. There is no disposition to examine the consequences. The program is maintained
by emotional support and too frequently enforced by
the approval of unthinking people who applaud it so
long as it does not include them. It is the type of domestic malpractice that the counselor will discover to
have been the cause of estrangement between parent
and child even more commonly than between husband
and wife. Whether he succeeds or not, it is his obligation to try to develop the insight or self-control that
will make the parent wiser or the spouse more restrained. As a matter of fact, the counselor very
quickly will discover that this apparent disregard of
self is essentially self-seeking, that it is motivated by
the effort to hold another captive. Especially is this
clear in the relationship of parents and children. The
recoil which the policy brings from its supposed bene-
ficiary is rooted in a fundamental self-defense on the
part of the child or spouse who realizes that he is being
made captive by what superficially appears as a mag-
nificent self-denial.

If the minister is constantly called upon to lessen
selfishness that is crudely and openly expressed, he is
more liable than many to a misinterpretation of a
parent's sacrifice and great generosity. If he becomes
an observing student of character, he will soon learn
through his counseling to be more searching in his
appraisal of motives and will, therefore, recognize in
most such cases that an underlying, concealed selfish-

ness may show itself in an expression of what, until it is analyzed and scrutinized, seems to be remarkable self-forgetting. Many times he will be forced to admit the unpleasant fact that he is being used as a counselor to justify or strengthen a life attitude that he is attempting, by his spiritual leadership, to eliminate from human life.

CHAPTER X

The Hazards of Domestic Counseling

THE minister, before he assumes the rôle of domestic counselor, needs to consider carefully the responsibilities involved in his acceptance of the confidences of those who come to him. First of all, he cannot safely function as a counselor unless he has a clear knowledge as to his legal responsibilities. His situation varies from state to state.

He may be so fortunate as to be privileged before the court, so that any confession that is made cannot be drawn from him by calling him to the witness stand. In many states, on the contrary, he has no such protection. He stands before the law as does any ordinary citizen.

Since lawyers predominate in our legislatures, they have taken care that they are free to function as counselors so that no legal pressure can ever be put upon them to force them to reveal what a client has said. The doctor sometimes enjoys the same freedom and, in some states, the priest and minister are equally fortunate. When this is not true, the minister must keep in mind, as he receives confidences, the possible legal liabilities that may be associated with the service he is attempting to perform.

Recently a friend of mine who, in his ministerial work, has developed rare skill in counseling found himself in a most embarrassing situation. In his effort to solve a family problem he had the husband and wife visit him. He was unable to lead them to a solution of their incompatibility. In the process of counseling with them, he listened, in the presence of the wife, to an unexpected confession by the husband concerning his marriage situation.

Later the wife sued for divorce and the minister was called to the witness stand to give testimony to what had occurred in his study. He refused to state what had been given him in confidence, explaining to the judge the predicament in which he found himself. He felt that if he rehearsed what the husband had said to him in strict confidence, his usefulness as a counselor was at an end. However, the law of the state gave only to the lawyer the privilege of withholding such information. The judge adjourned the court and pressure was put upon the minister to give the testimony which the wife's lawyer had depended upon for getting the divorce. The minister refused to change his position and was prepared to accept a jail sentence for contempt of court.

Fortunately, however, the woman's lawyer was a deacon in the church where the minister officiated. Eager as he was to get legal basis for the divorce, he was reluctant to put his own pastor in jail. A way was found to permit the minister to escape from his dilemma, and the question that would have led to the judge's declaration of contempt of court was not asked. It seemed clear in this case that the only thing that saved the minister was the fact that he happened to be the pastor of the church of the interested lawyer. Since, some years previously, a doctor who refused to give confidential information was sent to jail for several weeks by the same court, there appears little doubt that, had it been some other clergyman, he might have had to go to jail. If the minister had insisted that this confession should not be made in his presence, he would have been free from legal liability and could have handled the case just as effectively.

The minister must also, in his counseling, have regard for self-protection. No one who has had experience is likely to regard the task of the counselor lightly. One fact he has to keep in mind is that anything which leads to gossip and suspicion can be as deadly in its effect upon his career as proof of guilt. The greatest danger of counseling comes from those of neurotic constitution whose unsoundness shows itself in a peculiarly hazardous type of imagination. The risk would not be so great if people in general had any appreciation of the significance of what we know as a pathological liar. Few men and women realize the sort of irresponsibility that can make its own occasion for suspicion and choose an innocent victim for sacrifice.

Some years ago I received a letter from far-away Idaho. A woman wanted my help because she was being seriously injured by a man in her town who was doing evil things to her. Finally she explained that the man had an office opposite her residence and that she had never spoken to him, but nevertheless he was guilty of the most indecent attacks upon her. This was made possible by his thinking, the results of which she experienced. It was evident that this case revealed a mental abnormality in its early expression. The next step would have been an accusation that might have ruined a professional man who had never even spoken to the woman involved. An attempt was made to bring her to understand that she was suffering from an illness that led her to false thinking. Word also was sent at once to a prominent psychiatrist in the state who promised to attempt to get her to accept treatment and, if this failed, to keep an eye on the situation so that if the accusation broke into publicity his explanation of her irresponsibility would immediately follow.

Children are especially dangerous persons, and the minister who gives counsel to them must be thoroughly guarded. Very recently, the minister of a prominent local church was accused of rape by one of his Sunday school girls who had come to him for some rather unimportant advice. This case was sensibly handled. The girl was immediately examined and the physician reported that there was no possibility of her story being true. The frightening fact is, however, that had there been evidence of recent intercourse, although it was with someone else, there then would have been no way of demonstrating the innocence of the minister even though his conduct had been perfectly conventional.

The minister must also discipline himself so as not accidentally to betray confidences. He must be careful that there is no leaking through his wife. If she is a person who can maintain the same sense of responsibility as himself, he is fortunate and may wisely talk over with her his most serious problems. If, however, she is careless in repeating to her close friends information that she knows will greatly interest them, she is an unsafe partner in counseling. The minister must also look out that he does not let illustrations that may reveal confidences, or may be interpreted as doing so, slip into his sermonizing.

It is not easy to maintain anonymity in any report of a life situation. Some incidental detail may be sufficient to give a listener a clue to an entire situation. Recently, for example, in giving a very unusual, vivid illustration of a divorce situation while speaking to a class in a university in Florida, it became apparent to me that one of the students knew the family in New England of which I was speaking. After class I called her to me and she admitted the fact. I obtained her promise that for the welfare of those concerned she would never tell anyone the analysis of the situation that I had made. A happening like this shows that it is not even safe for the minister to refer to cases of previous years in other communities unless he is extremely careful to change the details that might lead someone to identify the people concerned.

Perhaps the minister's greatest danger comes from his natural impulse to talk over problems with friends whom he thinks he can trust. Although he may not give the names of the persons concerned, his hearers may recognize who these people are or may imagine that they know. These friends are more likely to disregard the minister's confidence than was he to disregard his parishioner's confidence. The third person may say something that starts dangerous gossip and may put an end to the minister's usefulness, and even make it difficult for him to establish himself in some other community.

It is important that the minister give some thought to the conditions under which he carries on his counseling. He must have privacy, but he must avoid isolation. If he has no secretary he had better not meet people in trouble in his church study but at his home and while his wife is in an adjoining room. To have regard for such matters may seem belittling to his profession, but, as a matter of fact, it is a sensible precaution. Since the doctor is not forgetful of the need of observing a similar care in his work, surely the minister, who is more open to attack, cannot wisely fail to provide the most propitious conditions possible for his counseling service.

The marriage counselor must always be on guard lest he be forced into the rôle of an advocate. He will find that a great many of those who come with the assertion that they wish help have an entirely different motive. They are not asking for insight, information or advice but are seeking someone who will agree with their own decision as to what should be done, and who will enlist in the effort to coerce the other person concerned to accept a ready-made solution. The marriage counselor must barricade himself against the extraordinary skill and emotional appeal which people have when they are determined to find an ally who will assist them in working out their purposes.

There are times when the marriage counselor finds that he is obligated to do something to influence a husband and wife so that a bad family situation may be corrected. Even so, he must make it clear to the other individual that he is not doing this as a champion, because of his personal attachment to the person who has come asking for assistance, or because he is fully converted to the interpretation he has received of the difficulty, but merely from his desire to bring a settlement that will be to the advantage of both persons. He cannot take on, as does the lawyer, the cause of one with disregard for the interests of the other. He wishes the welfare of both.

It must be remembered that the attempt to win an advocate takes not only subtle but even unconscious expression. People come with a thought-out program which may reveal great frankness. They also come with the belief that they are making a complete and unbiased presentation, when, as a matter of fact, they are driven to an intense partisanship by impulses that they have safely hidden from themselves. This emotional bias greatly complicates the problem of the counselor because often he can only with great difficulty get at the truth underneath the distortion of facts, which, with or without purpose, the person in trouble has set forth.

Experience helps the counselor in a surprising degree to develop a sort of scientific detection by which he penetrates the emotions but, even so, he can never have the assurance that comes to the physician who gathers information from objective experiments carried on in the laboratory. It is not that people are dishonest but rather that they find it almost impossible, in dealing with their own problems, to achieve honesty. We just have to take for granted that when emotions have command, the thinking process is tricked and becomes not a method of getting at truth but a process of finding reasons that justify the strong feeling.

The counselor must, if possible, gain the self-knowledge that makes him appreciate his own natural prejudices. It may be, for example, that he naturally tends to favor the woman when there is trouble between a man and his wife; it may be the other way. It also may be much more complex. Certain types may always quickly gain his sympathy while other personalities are handicapped in any statement of their problem because he is by impulse more critical concerning them. We may say that the counselor should be expected to be neutral because he has nothing at stake and therefore his judgments will always be objective. This, however, is fallacious. It assumes that the counselor brings to every domestic situation an intellectual attitude devoid of emotional presuppositions, preferences, or antipathies, and it is just this self-freedom that the individual cannot be counted upon to have as he attempts to analyze any concrete human situation. He, like others, is emotionally hampered by previous experience, and he must have sufficient self-understanding and discipline to achieve objectivity.

He must especially beware of any tendency to think through the problem by analogy, so that situations that are outwardly similar are regarded as having the same meaning, and a solution that worked in one case may be carried over to another. It is true, of course, that like cases do appear and that one experience helps the counselor to appreciate some other similar problem. If, however, the thinking process becomes an automatic classifying so that a routine procedure is developed and a standardized solution attempted, mischief may result.

Some years ago I helped a Christian worker rid himself forever of a fear he had that if he were alone his mind would turn to the thinking of vicious ideas that in his early youth had been the characteristic use of his imagination. He had unfortunately in late boyhood suffered serious warping of sex through the advances of a married woman. After a distinctly immoral late adolescence he married, became converted, and enlisted in a form of Christian service. Year after year, however, he carried the fear of relapsing into his former habits. Always he carried a book in his pocket, that he might, if he found himself alone, start reading to protect himself from his evil desire.

Finding that he was honest in his effort to be free from his trouble and discovering how intensely he loved his wife and how sincere he was in his religious thinking, I gave him counsel that to him seemed reckless and immoral. I told him henceforth to make no attempt to control his thinking. After some argument, merely because he had tried every other possible way out of his difficulty, I gained his promise that he would do at once what I had suggested. His surprise was great—so great indeed that he felt that something peculiar must have been done for him. Making no effort to control his mind, he discovered at once that he had no tendency whatever to take up the thinking in which he had reveled in the earlier part of his life. A year later he wrote me that he had never had any recurrence of his former tendency.

I explained to him that he had been fighting a shadow, that the substance of his difficulty had been melted away through his love of his wife and through his Christian service but that he had never been confident enough to test the strength of what once had been a dangerous enemy. Unfortunately I related this occurrence to a group of specialists in Christian service. Some months later, meeting one of them, I was told that he had come across the same kind of case, a student in one of the universities, and he had given the boy the advice that had worked so well in my case. I was shocked and terrified. The conditions of the two were, from every point of view, fundamentally different. One was married, the other unmarried. One was in the middle thirties; the other in the early twenties. One had developed strong domestic interests and a conscientious sense of parenthood, the other was in the formative period of late adolescence. Only on the surface was there any similarity. This mishap has taught me the necessity of always guarding myself from suggesting that an illustration reveals a technique. It merely discloses what worked well in a definite situation, and the procedure cannot, without great discrimination and diagnostic analysis, be carried over from one case and used in another in the effort to help someone who in many ways seems to be in the same predicament.

The marriage counselor also cannot become a mere classifier. There are those who attempt to do psychological service by having certain categories marked out, each labeled with scientific terminology. These persons operate by finding where any individual in trouble can be placed and on the basis of this diagnosis, routine counsel is given. In such instances there is no genuine individualizing of the problem, no serious effort to understand the person involved. Advice is given in a hit or miss fashion and the consequence may be that the client is hurt, not helped.

It is always the person who needs discovery and treatment. He does not conform to a scientific concept, however useful this may be in the field of science. He is a flesh-and-blood complex, a remarkably inconsistent personality, and no counselor can be of much service to him unless there is a willingness to attempt the exploration which the situation demands and the conditions permit.

The domestic counselor needs to be alert to the effects of fatigue. Although no condition has more influence over conduct, people in general do not consider, as they should, the consequences that come merely from getting tired. We live in an age when it is easy to overdraw one's capital of energy, and if it cannot be said that a great multitude are chronically overtired, it is no exaggeration to say that they are so close to this that any exceptional worry or conflict or exacting responsibility may push them over onto the wrong side of the line. The domestic counselor cannot safely forget that this condition of fatigue —and it is likely to be nervous rather than physical fatigue—is frequently the fundamental cause of trouble in marriage and family life. He will learn from experience that many difficulties clear up the moment the feeling of tension can be removed, and that this can only happen when the persons in trouble find some way to relax and rest.

Unfortunately, it is not easy for a person under strain to find a way to get the rest he needs. Merely ceasing from activity does not accomplish this. On the contrary, the mind may be all the freer to think the thoughts that rob the person of nervous energy even to the point of making sleep difficult or unprofitable. There are also frequently financial complications that make it useless for the counselor to suggest a vacation or a withdrawal from the strain existing in the family contacts. It will be apparent, however, that rest is the key to the situation. Fortunately, spiritual confidence, the optimism that is based upon a belief in the moral security of human life, does bring an assurance that lessens fatigue. At this point the minister will discover a therapeutic value in prayer, if only it can be genuine and bring a feeling of confidence through membership in the Kingdom of God.

The domestic counselor, however, is not interested in fatigue merely because it is one of the common causes of various sorts of maladjustment. He is also keenly attentive to the strain that shows itself during the period of counseling. It can be taken for granted in nearly all cases that the individual has not easily decided to go to somebody else for insight or direction. Putting aside the unemotional purposes that lead clients to the counselor's, such as the need of getting information, it must be assumed that there is a degree of tension even in the thought of carrying through a conference. If this has encouraged fatigue, the conferee will surely be influenced in his behavior, in what he says, and in how he says it during the conference. The probability is that this weariness will increase as the discussion proceeds. The counselor, therefore, must recognize that certain emotional exaggerations, extreme statements, weeping and the like may be, at least in part, the consequence of being tired. He must consider this as he interprets the conference. He should also do his utmost to prevent or lessen this exhaustion. If he can send the client away at the end of the conference feeling relieved, therefore less liable to fatigue, he has accomplished something important.

He will be influenced in what he says by the emotional state he recognizes in his clients. Neither in his manner nor in his work will he assume the impersonal, detached rôle of the judge, but he will cultivate a sensitiveness to the reactions of the client that is very similar to that of the doctor. He will be quick to end the conference when he finds that it is tiring the client to the point that makes it lose its value. He will also try to interpret, through such expressions of nervousness as may appear, the type of personality that has come to him.

To ignore the temperament of the individual would be disastrous. What we call the make-up of the person is a basic cause of his reactions and it must also be considered in any solution of the problem. The rapidity with which fatigue develops, the form it takes, and the influence it has over conduct are largely a matter of temperament. It is obvious that the more sensitive the person is, in the biological sense of awareness, the larger the response, the greater the liability of tension.

There can be, even here, no automatic program that the counselor can follow. He may be persuaded that the conference must be brief on account of the tired state of the client or he may be led to the conviction that there can be no lessening of stress or decrease of fatigue until the matter at issue is brought to some measure of settlement. The client must then be permitted to continue with the conference until there comes a glimmer of assurance or of insight which will permit the passing of the tension that is responsible for the fatigue. One thing is certain. No good comes from prolonging the conference if exhaustion has reached to the point that makes the mind of the client unable to function.

It will not do for the counselor to forget that he also is human, that he has a temperament that is expressed in his own reactions to strain. He may tire quickly and, if so, this must be taken into account as the conference proceeds. It may be that he has come to the appointment overtired and, therefore, is not in the best condition to guide the discussion. In any case he must learn not to allow other distressing problems to intrude as he supposedly gives his attention to the case at hand. Instead, for the welfare of those he seeks to help, he must try to train himself to give concentrated attention to each problem by itself. Once the interview is over, it should be crowded out of his mind—unless there is some purposeful investigation that he should make—as quickly and as thoroughly as possible. If counseling "gets on his nerves," as the saying is, so that he cannot keep his mind from rehearsing continuously a case in process and cannot prevent himself from awakening in the night and thinking over again the interview he has had, it would seem that either he is not a person who should assume the responsibilities of domestic counseling or that for some reason he is himself overtired and, therefore, thoroughly unfitted to deal with the tragedies of other people.

It is both wiser and more honorable for the counselor to recognize his limitations than to force upon himself services which should be turned over to someone else, either for the time being or always. In the latter case, of course, his pastoral service will have a lack but it will be better to accept this fact and strengthen his ministrations at other points than to try to do what fundamentally he is not equipped to undertake.

The marriage counselor must have a clearly defined policy regarding the responsibilities he is willing to assume. The family covers such a wide area of human interest that it is possible to include almost any sort of problem in his consultations if he so wills. Such a program is, however, hazardous and in the long run likely to bring him unpleasant consequences. For example, what should be his attitude toward problems that are essentially legal or medical? Good judgment will lead him away from ever taking over the responsibility for services that belong to the lawyer or the doctor. Indeed, he is doing an unlawful thing if he gives either legal or medical counsel. What, however, is more important is the fact that he is a layman in both of these fields, and yet, by giving advice, is daring to assume the prerogatives of the specialist. If some legal or medical question is involved in a problem that falls within his territory, he must insist that the client handle that part of his difficulty by enlisting the aid of a well qualified lawyer or physician.

This policy of restraint runs contrary to the recommendations of some ministers who have developed a reputation for domestic counseling. They believe that an exception should be made in regard to both mental and physical illness, because of the possibility of spiritual health. They report cases which they have handled successfully when they have acted as healers rather than as counselors. We have such evidence of apparent or actual healers of this sort that it does not seem reasonable to deny that there is such a thing as spiritual healing.

Although the scientist cannot claim to understand perfectly all these occurrences, there can be no doubt that suggestion is a large factor in bringing them about. We have cures from the use of patent medicine and apparatus that we know are, in fact, aside from the confidence or suggestion they bring, of no value whatsoever. In primitive life, illiterate people testify to cures brought about by medicine men and by various sorts of ceremonies. The question the domestic counselor needs to ask himself is not whether it will be possible for him occasionally to accomplish something that seems almost miraculous and which will be widely publicized in the community, by undertaking spiritual healing, or whether he will scrupulously restrain himself. If he is a wise man, he will not interpret domestic counseling in such a way as to permit himself to function as a spiritual healer.

He will not make this decision to deny people who seem to be, or are, physically or mentally ill the possibility of being helped or even cured by a spiritual ministration. No one who is in a position to give judgment would deny the therapeutic value of restoring spiritual confidence or moral harmony, and as a consequence removing the physical or psychic expression of inner stress and conflict. Nobody values these contributions from religion more than the psychiatrist who is familiar with human behavior.

The domestic counselor's program should exclude spiritual healing, not on account of scepticism, but because of his need to concentrate upon his proper function. Sensible people will surely discount his services if he attempts to spread himself and enter into every type of service where suggestion can be made to operate. In order to do his chosen task well, he needs to have a reputation for extraordinarily good judgment. It will be disastrous if he becomes known as a miracle man who has done remarkable things where the physician and the psychiatrist have failed.

Such publicity will soon force him out into the province in which he has intruded. More and more he will be confined to dealing with neurotic individuals, whose problems, for the most part at least, can be better handled by a physician or a psychiatrist. He will also soon arouse the suspicions of physicians and psychiatrists who can hardly regard him as anything other than a charlatan, because they accept a restraint which he does not. A physician, for example, increasingly hesitates to take over a problem that is clearly psychic. A psychiatrist who assumes responsibility for medical advice, even though he has a medical degree, is making a grave mistake.

I remember Dr. Frankwood E. Williams, who did so much to develop mental hygiene in the United States, telling me once that somebody who was a psychiatric patient of his claimed to have a sore throat. She said, "Dr. Williams, won't you please see what is the matter with my throat?" Immediately, he dismissed her and told her to go to the proper specialist, saying that under no circumstances would he mix up medical treatment with the psychiatric. He was, however, well trained in general medicine since he was, of course, a graduate of one of our best medical schools. Telling me of this incident, he said that nothing would destroy his influence as a psychiatrist so quickly as catering to the wishes of his patients that he also become their physician.

Those ministers who have a conviction that they should assume responsibility for spiritual healing ought to regard it as an art in itself. The domestic counselor should stick to his knitting, because he is a realist and appreciates the necessity of establishing himself as an unusually level-headed, fact-facing individual who does not cultivate the mysterious and the occult. If, in domestic counseling, he does happen to bring about cures in persons who have, or seem to have, physical or psychic maladies, he will take great care not to emphasize this or allow it to become a means of advertising him as a possessor of some special gift.

Domestic counseling offers a field of service large enough for professionally ambitious persons. There should be no temptation to become a sort of psychic jack-of-all-trades. This self-imposed limitation does not, of course, mean that the counselor should not be a student of human conduct, as it is expressed outside his special interest. On the contrary, he cannot function with his greatest efficiency unless he reads as widely as time and circumstances permit in the literature that deals with human behavior. No subject of study can be more fascinating or more sure to convince him that the ways in which people react are as varied as the kinds of problems with which they struggle. He will not be intolerant in his attitude toward other kinds of service, but will accept the discipline and specialization that become the obligation of anyone who takes over a particular professional responsibility.

BIBLIOGRAPHY

References to Part I

Brunner, Emil. *The Divine Imperative*. London: The Lutterworth Press.

Cabot, Richard C. *Christianity and Sex*. New York: The Macmillan Company.

Calverton, V. F. and S. D. Schmalhausen (Editors). *Sex in Civilization*. New York: The Macaulay Company.

Crombie, Frederick. *The Writings of Origen*. Two Volumes. Edinburgh: T. and T. Clark.

Cross, Earle Bennett. *The Hebrew Family*. Chicago: The University of Chicago Press.

Elliott-Binns, L. E. *The Church in the Ancient World*. London: John Heritage, The Unicorn Press.

Ellwood, Charles A. *The World's Need of Christ*. New York: Abingdon-Cokesbury Press.

Glover, T. R. *The Conflict of Religions in the Early Roman Empire*. Ninth Edition. London: Methuen and Company, Ltd.

Goodsell, Willystine. *A History of Marriage and the Family*. Revised Edition. New York: The Macmillan Company.

Halliday, W. R. *The Pagan Background of Early Christianity*. Liverpool: The University Press of Liverpool, Ltd.

Hannay, James O. *The Spirit and Origin of Christian Monasticism*. London: Methuen and Company, Ltd.

Hart, Hornell and Ella B. Hart. *Personality and the Family*. Revised Edition. Boston: D. C. Heath and Company.

Lecky, William Edward Hartpole. *History of European Morals*. New York: Longmans, Green and Company.

Ligon, Ernest M. *The Psychology of Christian Personality*. New York: The Macmillan Company.

Lindsay, A. D. *The Moral Teaching of Jesus*. New York: Harper and Brothers, Publishers.

Main, John. *Religious Chastity*. New York.

McGiffert, Arthur Cushman. *A History of Christianity in the Apostolic Age*. Revised Edition. New York: Charles Scribner's Sons.

Moffatt, James. *The First Five Centuries of the Church*. Nashville: Cokesbury Press.

Piper, Otto A. *The Christian Interpretation of Sex*. New York: Charles Scribner's Sons

Schaff, Philip (Editor). *A Select Library of the Nicene and Post Nicene Fathers*. Volume VI, St. Jerome *Letters*. New York: Charles Scribner's Sons.

Schmiedeler, Edgar. *Christian Marriage*. Washington, D. C.: The Catholic Conference on Family Life.

——————. *An Introductory Study of the Family*. New York: The Century Company.

——————. *The Sacred Bond*. New York: P. J. Kenedy and Sons.

Scott, William. *A History of the Early Christian Church*. Nashville: Cokesbury Press.

Sherrill, Lewis Joseph. *The Family and Church*. New York: The Abingdon Press.

Tertullian. *Letter to His Wife*. Letter XI. Volume XI of the *Ante Nicene Christian Library*. New York: Christian Literature Company.

Uhlhorn, Gerbard. *The Conflict of Christianity With Heathenism*. New York: Charles Scribner's Sons.

Wand, J. W. C. *A History of the Early Church to A. D. 500*. London: Methuen and Company, Ltd.

Wieman, Regina Westcott. *The Modern Family and the Church*. New York: Harper and Brothers.

References to Part II

Adamson, Elizabeth I. *So You're Going to a Psychiatrist*. New York: Thomas Y. Crowell Company.

Adler, Alfred. *The Neurotic Constitution*. New York: Moffat, Yard and Company.

————. *The Practice and Theory of Individual Psychology*. New York: Harcourt, Brace and Company.

Baker, Harry J. *The Art of Understanding*. Boston: The Christopher Publishing House.

Burnham, William H. *The Wholesome Personality*. New York: D. Appleton and Company.

Cowles, Edward Spencer. *Don't Be Afraid!* New York: Whittlesey House.

Edwards, Richard Henry. *A Person-Minded Ministry*. Nashville: Cokesbury Press.

Freud, Sigmund. *The Future of an Illusion*. New York: Horace Liveright and the Institute of Psycho-Analysis.

————. *A General Introduction to Psychoanalysis*. New York: Horace Liveright.

————. *New Introductory Lectures on Psycho-Analysis*. New York: W. W. Norton and Company, Inc.

Groves, Catherine. *Get More Out of Life*. New York: Association Press.

Groves, Ernest R. *Understanding Yourself*. Second Edition. New York: Emerson Book Company.

Groves, Ernest R. and Phyllis Blanchard. *Readings in Mental Hygiene*. New York: Henry Holt and Company.

Jung, C. G. *Modern Man in Search of a Soul*. New York: Harcourt, Brace and Company, Inc.

————. *Psychological Types*. New York: Harcourt, Brace and Company, Inc.

————. *Psychology of the Unconscious*. New York: Moffat, Yard and Company.

Mackenzie, Murdo. *The Human Mind*. Philadelphia: The Blakeston Company.

May, Rollo. *The Art of Counseling*. Nashville: Cokesbury Press.

Preu, Paul William. *Outline of Psychiatric Case-Study*. New York: Paul B. Hoeber, Inc.

Rank, Otto. *Truth and Reality*. New York: Alfred A. Knopf.

————. *Will Therapy*. New York: Alfred A. Knopf.

Shaffer, Laurance Frederic. *The Psychology of Adjustment*. New York: Houghton Mifflin Company.

Stolz, Karl Ruf. *Pastoral Psychology*. Revised Edition. Nashville: Abingdon-Cokesbury Press.

Travis, Lee Edward and Dorothy Walter Baruch. *Personal Problems of Everyday Life*. New York: D. Appleton-Century Company.

Wallin, J. E. Wallace. *Minor Mental Maladjustments in Normal People*. Durham: Duke University Press.

Weatherhead, Leslie D. *Psychology in Service of the Soul*. New York: The Macmillan Company.

INDEX

Accusation, 205

Acts of Paul and Thekla, The,
54

Adolescent group, 115

Aged people, 120

Alliance of family and church,
65

Anonymity, 206; city, 138

Apostolic period, 63

Asceticism, 39; Catholic attitude toward, 57, 58; Christianity's struggle with, 29; ebb
and flow of, 63; influences
leading to, 43; modern attitude toward, 62, 63; philosophy of life, 30

Attitudes, morbid, 100

Beaven, Albert W., vi

Bibliography, 221

Body demand, early Christian
attitude toward, 38, 39

Brooks, Bishop Phillips, 29, 58,
169

Browning, Robert, 194

Brunner, Emil, 60

Cana, wedding at, 30

Case, follow up of, 132; outcome of, 137

Catholic church, asceticism special liability of, 56

Catholic priest, 140

Causal influences of childhood,
12

Celibacy, Catholic attitude toward, 58, 59

Child, influence upon parent,
28, 29; training, 120

Children, dangerous persons,
205

Christian, living, onwardness of,
9; marriage, 58; way of life,
8, 12, 24

Christianity, backward movements, 9; first expression of,
63; history of, 20; mission of,
76, 79

Church, mission of, 26; school,
115

Church fathers, 44; writings of,
40

Circulating library, 126

Classifier, 212

Colgate-Rochester Divinity
School, The, vi

Commandments, The, 68

Conference, 189

Confession, 145

Consultations, several, 193

Conybeare, F. C., 54

Correspondence, 152

Counseling, privacy of conditions, 207; special service, 136

Counselor, a prop, 154; technique of, 155

Courage, source of, 153

Critical attitude, 184

Data, useful, 75

Dearborn, Lester, 121

Definite problem, 170

Discipline, as professional responsibility, 220

Divine Imperative, The, 60

Divorce, 98, 106, 198, 203

Domestic, association, 73; counsel, 128; counselors, different backgrounds of, 129; fulfillment, 80; relations, science of, 112, 117; values, 80

Dominant materialism, 83

Earl of Shaftesbury, 12

Early Christianity, chief task of, 41

Emotional maturity, 72

Essenes, 43

Eve, 53

Examination, medical, 135

Experience, individualizing of, 94

Extravertive, bombardment, 91; emphasis, 87; exaggeration, 91

Family, advantage of, 25; alliance between church, vii; ally of Christianity, 24; attitude toward, 23; childless, 95; fellowship, 74; function of, 11, 25; importance of, 3; importance of in program of Christianity, 5; literature of, 125; maturing influence of, 72; microcosm, 65; particularizing of, 109; pattern, 76; relationship to Christianity, 4, 66; service of, 24, 25; spiritual aspect of, 65; spiritual significance of, 26; three interests of, 27; wholesomeness of, 30

Fatigue, 212, 213

Fictitious spiritual achievement, 66

Fidelity, 107

First Corinthians, 46, 48

Freud, Sigmund, 33, 52

Gethsemane, meaning of struggle, 20

God, concept of, 17; fatherhood of, 11; household of, 22; Jesus' interpretation of, 18; kingdom of, 18, 43, 49; relationship of man to, 16, 17

Goodsell, Willystine, 25

Gratitude, 150

Greek tragedies, 143

Guilt, 188; sense of, 132

Hannay, James O., 56, 62

Hardship standards, 81

Hawthorne, Nathaniel, 160

Healers, 217

Hebrews, 54

Hellenistic mysticism, 50

Henry, George W., 59

History of Christianity in the Light of Modern Knowledge, 16

History of Marriage and the Family, 25

Home, importance of, 11; meaning of, 24; spiritual significance of, 27; standardized, 108

Home life, relationship between religion and American, v

Home nursery, 77

Illusive element, 70

"Illusiveness of Life," 71

Illustration, case for, 151

Immaturity, emotional, 98

Index system, card, 139

Individual, Jesus' interest in, 67, 68; sacredness of, 66; sensitiveness of, 145; uniqueness of, 70, 164

Individualism, domestic, 69

Infant damnation, 77

Information, giver of, 152

Instruction, medical school, 35

Interests, externalizing of, 86
Interview, 182
Introductory Study of the Family, An, 59
Introvertive experience, necessity of, 49

Jack-of-all-trades, psychic, 220
Jehovah, 19
Jesus, boyhood of, 15; commanding motive of, 6; conflict with orthodox religious leaders, 17; disciples of, 19, 20; doctrine of, 5, 18; genius of teachings, 5; home life of, 13; illustrations of, 13; many-sidedness of the teaching, 4; teachings of, 10, 11, 14, 22, 27; terminology of, 13; unmarried status of, 30, 31; use of family experience, 10; way of life, 4, 5, 7, 15, 72
Jewish family, strength of, 15, 16
Jews, faith of, 17
John, 68
Jung, C. G., 33

Lecky, William E. H., 56
Lectures, 116
Legal responsibilities, 202
Leisure, misuse of, 93
Life, history, 160; inner, 88, 90
Listener, 144
Little Theatre, 92
Love, among family members, 6; higher type of, 6; interpretation of, 6; passion distinguished from, 34; power of, 6; propulsion of, 6; self-renewal of, 9; survival purpose of, 7
Luke, 14
Luther, 57

Man, brotherhood of, 11
Marble Faun, The, 160
Mark, 4, 14, 68, 69
Marriage, adjustment, 119; Jesus' approval of, 31; literature of, 125; Paul's approval of, 31; scriptural anchorage of, 64
Matthew, 64, 67, 77
Mechanisms of Character Formation, 75
Minister, 205; a conciliator, 156; an interpreter, 151; overidealizing of, 147; Protestant, 159; silent partner, 154; young, 168
Minister's wife, 206
Monuments of Early Christianity, 54
Moody, D. L., 169
Mother-child attitude, 77
My Father's House, 26

National Conference on Family Relations, 117
New books, 126
Noyes, Pierrepont, 26

Objective, need of being, 167
Occult, 220
Old Testament, concepts and sentiments of, 17; designations of, 17
Oneida Community, experiences of, 25, 26
One person's side, 195

Paganism, 79
Pamphlets and articles, 126
Parent, influence upon child, 28, 29
Parental affection, 7, 8
Parent-child association, 7, 8
Parenthood, indictment of, 27; side-stepping of, 94
Passion, love distinguished from, 34

Paul, 43, 50, 51, 54; core of teachings, 49; ideas toward marriage, 45, 46, 47, 48; unmarried status of, 30, 31
Personal conference, 118
Personal ethics, problem of, 140
Physical examination, 174
Pictures, motion, 89
Pius XI, 58
Pliny the Younger, 44
Political kingdom, preconception of, 19, 20
Political triumph, 20
Pregnancy, 119
Prejudices, 209
Problem, fictitious, 143
Protestant, the, 111
Pseudo-scientists, 133, 134
Psychiatrists, interests of, 171
Psychic midwife, 156
Psychoanalyst, 149, 171
Publicity, 219

Rapport, 173
Rauschenbusch Foundation, vi
Recently married, 115
References to Part I, 221
References to Part II, 223
Religious leadership, helping, 86
Revelation, 64
Robertson, Frederick, 71
Roman Empire, 43, 44
Roman life, Christian interpretation of, 44, 45
Roman people, moral decline of, 44
Russia, 69

Sacramental grace, doctrine of, 58
Sacrifice hit, 157
Samaria, woman of, 67
Sayre, Paul, 116
Schmiedeler, Edgar, 58, 59
Science, 82

Searching, polygamous, 99
Second visit, 133
Self-deception, 184
Self-decision, 189
Self-defense, 197
Self-discovery, 186
Self-elimination, campaign of, 155
Self-interest, 199
Self-interpretation, 187
Self-knowledge, 190
Self-protection, 204
Sermonizing, 114, 115
Sex, ascetic attitude toward, 31, 32; Christian attitude toward, 50, 51, 52, 53; emphasis upon, 61; false Christian attitude toward, 60; function of reproduction, 31, 32; indictment by church, 27; overemphasis on, 96; part in husband-wife fellowship, 32; personal response of, 35; physiological and nervous significance of, 40; relationship to love, 61, 62; spiritual significance of, 33; suspicion of Christian leadership toward, 37; variants, 59
Sex impulse, 99; ascetic attitude toward, 39; hazard of, 37; influence on religion, 38; normal expression of, 54, 55; social conditioning of, 55; social dependence of, 50
Shakers, the, 27, 57
Social relationship, meaning of, 7
Specialists, 113
Spirit and Origin of Christian Monasticism, The, 56, 62
Spiritual, fellowship, realization of, 26; healing, 220, 221; perversion, appearance of, 20; values, 84
Subjective facts, 149

Suggestion, 158, 190, 218
Superior family, 85
Superiority, 181, 182
Sympathy, 178, 179, 180

Teaching program, purpose of, 110
Tolstoy, 59
Temperament, 215
Tension, conference, 214

Unconscious expression, 208
Updegraph, Leslie, 121

Virginity, Christian attitude toward, 54

Watts, William E., 121
White, William A., 75
Williams, Frankwood E., 219
Woman of Samaria, Jesus' conversation with, 67

Young Men's Christian Association of Boston, 120
Y Paterquiz, The, 124